MARKETING
SAVES THE WORLD

———

a memoir

HOW TO SELL CHARITY, CONSULTING AND CAPITALISM

Redefining what people value

BILL MATASSONI

A Kris Safarova | StrategyTraining.com & Firmsconsulting Original

MARKETING SAVES THE WORLD

a memoir

© 2017 by Bill Matassoni

A Kris Safarova | StrategyTraining.com & Firmsconsulting Original

November 2019

2ND EDITION

Published & Printed in the United States of America by Firmsconsulting LLC, a member of the Strategy Media Group LLC, Los Angeles, group of companies.

www.firmsconsulting.com

Firmsconsulting and The Strategy Media Group are registered trademarks of The Strategy Media Group.

Firmsconsulting business books are available at special discounts for bulk purchases for sales promotions or corporate use. Special editions, including personalized covers, excerpts of existing books, or books with corporate logos can be created in large quantities for specific needs. For more information, please contact Kris Safarova at **kris@firmsconsulting.com**.

FIRMSCONSULTING L.L.C.

187 E. Warm Springs Rd.
Suite B158
Las Vegas, NV 89119
info@firmsconsulting.com

Disclaimer: This work contains general information only and is not intended to be construed as rendering accounting, business, financial investment, legal, tax, or other professional advice and/or services. This work is not a substitute for such professional advice and services, nor should it be used as a basis for any decision or action that may affect your business and/or career. The author and publisher disclaim any liability, loss, or risk that is incurred as a consequence of the use and applications of any of the contents of this work.

ISBN 978-1-7340327-0-3

THE BILL MATASSONI SHOW

**Would you like to receive a complimentary episode
of The Bill Matassoni Show?**

Shot on location in a beautiful Philip Johnson New Canaan Glass House featured prominently in the memoir. Bill hosts a twenty-episode documentary series providing additional insights and explanations to support the central premise of his memoir. Go to:

www.MarketingSavesTheWorld.com

LIMITED EDITION
MEMOIR

What if a book were not just a book? What if the book enabled the reader to understand the concept of spaces and dimensions before reading a word? The hand-built memoir does just that.

A SWASHBUCKLING
ADVENTURE

———

eVERY NOW AND THEN someone comes along whose treatment of the subject of management is both entertaining and insightful. That's what Bill Matassoni has accomplished in his memoir, which covers his forty-year career selling what he calls "ephemeral things."

Bill, a former McKinsey and BCG partner, distills his life, loves and lessons in this unique story of the evolution of the modern marketer. He presents an entirely new way to think about unlocking value in market-spaces, not places. He recounts his adventures—and they are adventures—working for The United Way of America, McKinsey, BCG, Ashoka and other organizations. In all of them, ideas were the product and emotion was as important as reason. We learn about how Victoria's Secret "democratized" luxury, why beer might become a nutritional product, how BCG tried to compete with McKinsey and the growing impact of social entrepreneurs. Marketing Saves the World teaches us how to find new dimensions of value that make the world better by enabling multiple stakeholders to win. It is about capitalism with a capital "C." Says Bill, "Forget about sharing the pie. Make it bigger."

Kris Safarova

THIS MEMOIR IS DEDICATED
TO PAMELA VALENTINE

———

Also known as Slim. She's the best thing that's ever happened to me.
I asked her to marry me two weeks after I met her. She says I didn't.
What I said was, "Damn it, I'm in love with you." She doesn't understand
marketing. More about all that later.

Then felt I like some watcher of the skies
  When a new planet swims into his ken;
Or like stout Cortez, when with eagle eyes
  He stared at the Pacific—and all his men
Look'd at each other with a wild surmise—
  Silent, upon a peak in Darien.

Keats: On First Looking into Chapman's Homer

CONTENTS

1

PREFACE

WHY READ THIS BOOK? Well, for one thing it's short—about the length of an average plane ride. It doesn't require careful study. To paraphrase Samuel Johnson, it tries to balance entertainment with instruction. It's a memoir—a rags-to-riches account of being in the right places at the right times. There is some casual theory about marketing. For example, how to persuade someone to treat an incurable disease, how to get a person to give to a charity or how to convince a successful CEO to spend large amounts of money on a consulting engagement. I've done all that and discovered things that work. They're worth learning. If you can sell this soft stuff well, you can sell the hard stuff even better.

My story also makes a case that marketing, more than finance and strategy, is an essential ingredient for the success of companies and their leaders. That if you become good at marketing, you will make lots of money and actually enjoy your career. Marketing is fun and gives you the chance to be the kind of person people want to have around.

That said, people are suspicious of marketing because it is as much art as science and there's lots of room to hide laziness and incompetence in the art part. The skeptics will invariably demand careful thinking from you and you will be asked to deliver measurable results.

Moreover, you will need to be determined not to let your vision be confined by established definitions of what clients and consumers want. Marketing should be more highly regarded, and it will be if marketers get better at identifying new dimensions of value. What will those dimensions be? Which ones will last for a decade or longer? Luxury, convenience, intelligence, mobility, community? You tell me. There are forces at work in the world that will make new and almost unthinkable dimensions possible.

Beyond that, my short treatise argues that marketing can make a big difference in the world. I have been fortunate to have had an unusual career that has covered the private and non-profit sectors. I've run marketing at one of the world's biggest charities and was the partner for marketing and brand at two major consulting firms. My experiences have convinced me that marketing is really systems redesign and it can solve seemingly intransigent social and environmental problems that too often and unnecessarily pit interest groups against each other. Marketing, not diplomacy or negotiating skills, can resolve conflicts and actually create immense value rather than make compromises that merely share the pie as it currently exists.

In healthcare, the environment, education and other areas, marketers have a big role to play in helping us redefine our objectives and the dimensions of value over which we should compete and cooperate. Think about that farmer in rural India who needs to know what makes him sick. Cost really isn't the problem. The problem is he doesn't have the time to walk for a day to get to a distant hospital. He needs blood tests in a box delivered through franchises that look like McDonald's or Starbucks. That's what marketing can do. That's what marketing is doing. Think about the pipeline for Alzheimer's drugs. It's nearly empty because the approval system for new drugs is broken. We need to reinvent that system with new policies, decisions, levels and flows. That is what marketers can do and have done. Think about the student with great grades who can't pursue her education without taking on big debts. Think about the investor who can't find decent returns without taking big risks. What if he could invest in her and be paid a small percentage of her future earnings? That's now happening in several countries in South America. That's now happening because of a marketer.

There are some experts who say that someday soon consumers in advanced economies will have everything they need. How foolish. That will happen only if regulation and policy add transaction costs that make markets stagnant. Or, even worse, it could happen if marketers lack the imagination to see new places where value can be created.

If none of this piques your interest, then don't read any further. But you will miss some good stories about lingerie, beer and bug spray. To say nothing of my 1967 Mustang convertible with the fur-covered seats.

2

NEVER!
UNLESS IT'S
CHOICE STUFF

Y GRADES at Harvard Business School were fine, even respectable, but not good enough to attract McKinsey's attention when I graduated in 1975. McKinsey, the prestigious strategy consulting firm, took its pick from among the top performers in each class. Yet, just a few years later, in 1979, McKinsey asked me twice to join them to create and run its marketing function. I turned them down the first time. I said something like, "Look, I'm making 40k a year, driving a '67 Mustang convertible and dating a Dallas Cowboys cheerleader. And besides, I really like being the head of marketing for a big charity." The recruiter on the other end of the phone line went silent. He must have thought I was nuts.

I wasn't nuts, but I had not figured out what I wanted to do with my life. I was a coal miner's son who made it to and through college on scholarships. I had a great time, but I didn't get the memo about figuring out a career. So, after graduating I taught school for a few years, then sold stocks and bonds. Then I applied to Harvard Business School. I felt I needed to do something to build a base. It was last minute, but I got in. Mitt Romney was in my class. George W. Bush and I wrote a paper together.

Business school was tolerable but not compelling. I really didn't find management and business interesting—certainly less interesting than the mathematics and literature I studied at Harvard College. When I graduated from HBS, my wife at the time forbade me to take a job in New York City. Looking elsewhere, I got one, and only one, offer—from a beltway bandit consulting firm in Washington D.C. My first assignment was to analyze the effects of oil well brine reinjection on the safety of drinking water. You know, brine reinjection. When I turned in my report after three months of working alone, the only comment I got was I should have double-spaced it. I resigned.

Then lightning struck. A friend told me about a marketing firm she had encountered. She thought I might fit in. "They're different and you're different." Jack Porter and Bill Novelli founded and ran the firm. They both had been successful New York ad men, but they decided they wanted to do something good for the world and saw social marketing as a way to do it. Their firm, Porter Novelli, had clients such as the National Cancer Institute and the National High Blood Pressure Education Program. Social marketing is just like regular marketing except behavior is more important than money. You pay for some benefit—or cure—with your behavior or lifestyle rather than cash. Of course, you may have to buy drugs to treat whatever is trying to kill you or causing you pain, but that is a small part of the contract.

I liked the idea of what Porter Novelli did. It wasn't just business and numbers. I met Novelli and we hit it off. We were both, after all, poor Italian kids from western Pennsylvania. We played soccer and, of course, we were crazy fans of the Pittsburgh Steelers. No surprise, I got the job. I spent the next two years learning how to convince people to keep treating their high blood pressure. Detection wasn't the issue. Recidivism was the problem. People stopped taking their drugs, started eating too much salt again, regained the weight they had lost, etc. It was a tough sell telling people they had an incurable disease that was probably going to kill them and all they could do to prolong their lives was change their lifestyle.

I read everything I could to get some insight. A book titled *Compliance with Therapeutic Regimens* became my bible. I learned how reinforcement by pharmacists and nurses was vital, much more important than doctors' warnings. I learned that compliance was a daily sale or "repeat purchase" and I tried to convince our government clients that their goal was compliance rather than detection and awareness. That the value their program created was determined not by increased awareness, but by the number of people who became aware they had high blood pressure and did what they needed to do to lower it and keep it low.

To no avail. The clients were government bureaucrats, mostly. To them, the big goal was detection and the big event was National High Blood Pressure Education Month and the poster that went with it. That was my job. Forget the theory. Novelli gave me a challenge. He said, "Let's come up with three posters. Make one really safe. Then, try something new with the second. And do something crazy with the third." We brainstormed about the themes of the poster and came up with two. One was health, of course. The other was, well, love. Treat your high blood pressure because people love you, and you them.

So, there I was in front of about 40 people presenting my three posters. Novelli was in the front row next to the head of the program, who was, as usual, enjoying a can of Orange Crush. I greeted everyone and unveiled the first, safe poster. There in big bold letters it said, "High Blood Pressure Can't Be Cured. You Need to Treat It, Every Day."

Silence. Not disapproval. Just silence.

So I went to the second poster and turned it around on its easel. There was a picture of an African-American man with a big smile on his face. Almost beaming. (African-Americans are particularly susceptible to high blood pressure.) The poster read, "Perform an Act of Love Today, Treat Your High Blood Pressure."

A little more interest, but some skepticism that compliance and love had much to do with each other. It was time. I walked over to the third poster and turned it around. Same beaming face. The copy read, "You are an Eagle. You are a Rock! You Fly with the Hopes of the People Who Love You. You are the Earth on Which They Rest. Treat Your High Blood Pressure."

I looked at the group. Novelli had a big grin on his face. The head of the program leaned back in his chair. It was a little over the top for him.

We went with option two. At least we convinced our client that the frame of our communications needed to change. It couldn't be about health. It needed to be about love and responsibility to your family. What I learned from the experience is you need to look for new dimensions and that often those dimensions can be very different from what currently sells your product. But what I didn't learn then was new dimensions require more than just a new business model. They require you to change your identity.

By dimension, I don't mean something as precise as the word's meaning in mathematics. But I mean more than a new angle or niche that increases sales. I mean a genuine change in direction and a re-definition of value. Something that drives everything else and defines benefit. The proximity rather than the cost of healthcare in rural areas is an example. So is respect for people's dying wishes in palliative care. On a more prosaic level, durability instead of density in a software chip. Handling and tread life in a tire. For me, dimension has come to be a powerful way of looking at—and actually seeing—a new marketing space and challenge.

New dimensions can create new markets or make your target customers much more clearly defined. Think of a matrix for people with high blood pressure. The horizontal, or x-axis, is unaware/aware.

The vertical, or y-axis, is not treat and treat. Treatment needed to be a bigger part of our message both to reinforce and regain the right behavior. To get people to stay on treatment, we added a third dimension: emotion and love of family.

We did manage to have some fun selling compliance. Jimmy the Greek, the famous Las Vegas odds-maker, agreed to do a public service announcement for the program. We shot him walking through the halls of the National Institutes of Health saying something like, "Hi, I'm Jimmy the Greek. I make my living making bets. But there is one thing I won't bet on. That's my blood pressure. Know your numbers." That wasn't the fun part. Jimmy did the spot in one take. Afterwards, he says to me and Graham, the head of the program, "How was that? Was it good for you?" We nod our heads. He says, "That's terrific. Hey, let's have drinks and dinner tonight."

"Sure Jimmy, that sounds great."

Jimmy says, "I'm staying in a suite at the Four Seasons in Georgetown. Meet me there at seven."

We get to the suite, Jimmy opens the door; he's dressed in a purple smoking jacket. Purple. "Graham, Bill, hey come on in. What do you have? Bourbon, beer, wine?"

"Orange Crush," says Graham. Jimmy has a hard time finding the Crush in the bar. I pour myself a bourbon, a big one.

"That was a lot of fun today. A lot of fun. Thanks for joining me," says Jimmy. "You guys married, have girlfriends?"

"Married."

"Girlfriends."

He smiles. "Yeah, it's great to be married. I love my wife. Love my wife." Takes a drink.

"Fool around much?" There's a pause. We both say no.

"Nah, I don't either," (longer pause), "...unless it's choice stuff."

Right then and there, I knew it was going to be an interesting night. To this day, my wife and I joke about that line. Whenever one of us says "never," we pause and say, "unless it's choice stuff."

One early summer morning, not long after that, a large man showed up at Porter Novelli's offices in Georgetown. He was dressed entirely in black and mostly leather. Who does this guy think he is? Federico Fellini? Close. His name was Mario Pellegrini and he was from the United Way. I went out to greet him. "Mario, thank you for coming, but I would have been happy to come to Alexandria and meet you at the United Way headquarters."

"Thanks, but I can't go back there. My wife might serve me with divorce papers."

Mario had conceived and sold to the National Football League a rather remarkable idea. Pete Rozelle and the NFL had negotiated a deal with the networks to broadcast their games. Part of the deal gave the NFL one minute of every game to broadcast whatever they wanted. As a result, they were getting bombarded with requests for this "free" time, mostly by philanthropic organizations. Mario convinced the NFL to give all the time to United Way. That way, they could greatly simplify things by saying United Way helps hundreds of organizations across the U.S. By helping United Way, we help them all. Mario offered to produce a television spot for every team featuring one of its players.

When Novelli told me this, I asked, "Why is he coming to us?" We are a social marketing firm. He should go to an ad firm. Novelli looked at me and said, "Bill, his name is Pellegrini. Mine is Novelli. And yours is Matassoni. What more do I need to explain?"

So my new client was United Way of America and my job was to write and help produce dozens of 30- and 60-second television and radio spots that were carried on all nationally and locally broadcast games. And the playoffs and the Super Bowl. In terms of exposure for United Way, it was a huge campaign worth millions of dollars. United Way paid for the production. We had a tight budget because we needed to film in every NFL city. Writing the spots themselves was relatively straightforward.

Player on camera: "Hi, my name is --------. I play -----for the --- -------. This is a great city for football. If you come here, be sure to visit the ------ and the -----. People here love their town and feel an obligation to each other. That's why we all support our local United Way. The -----United Way, with your financial help, supports ------different social and health organizations dedicated to helping people who need their help. Organizations such as the Boys Club, the Cancer Society, the ------- and the-----. My teammates and I all support our United Way. Remember, thanks to you, it works for all of us."

For the most part, the players did a good job even though they were not used to speaking on camera in a suit and tie. The NFL's SVP of marketing, Joe Browne, picked all the players. I remember one day in Los Angeles at a modest studio on La Brea Avenue we filmed Jack Youngblood, Ahmad Rashad (then still known as Bobby Moore) and Jim Zorn. They all did great with Mario's help. Rashad was a standout. Afterwards, Joe and I were sitting outside on the sidewalk waiting for the crew to pack up. It must have been 90 degrees. It was a Sunday. Joe said to me, "So, Mr. Harvard, how long are you going to work for United Way? This isn't what you guys usually do."

"I don't know. How long are you going to work at the league?"

"I don't know."

Joe had started in the mailroom at the NFL. He ended up working closely with Pete Rozelle, Paul Tagliabue and Roger Goodell and was on a first-name basis with over half the NFL owners. He retired last year and 15 owners came to his farewell dinner.

Filming didn't always go smoothly. One player–a smart, highly regarded player–had to do 33 takes of "Hi, my name is -----." He was just nervous.

I usually tried to keep the copy simple. For one spot on mental illness, I got a little carried away. We filmed it in Malibu on the beach. We used a kite in the wind to symbolize the ups and downs of depression. Our player was a Rhodes Scholar. In pre-production, the day before, everything worked perfectly. It was sunny and windy. The next day was bleak and calm and the kite kept falling onto the beach. That affected the player, who stumbled through his lines. My guess is he felt that he, a quarterback, should be perfect in one take. He put too much pressure on himself and my convoluted script didn't help. We ended up taping him in a nearby hotel room and dubbing the spot.

One time a local PR guy substituted a player for the team spot. He didn't tell Joe. We showed up early on a Saturday morning in New Orleans. It was humid and overcast. As we set up, the player arrived. He was huge and unshaven. No tie or jacket. We helped him shave in a public fountain and got him a jacket, but he still looked pretty rough. Worse, the spot was on how the local United Way was helping battered women. Still worse, the player had a very hard time reading the teleprompter. He was the first to say that maybe we should find someone else on his team to represent the NFL. He apologized. I felt bad for him. It wasn't fair and Joe let the local PR guy know it.

Sometimes recipients of the help provided by United Way agencies appeared in the spots. In one spot, a particularly elegant and articulate player was sitting next to an old man who suffered from dementia. Every time the player got halfway into the script, the man would shout, "Thanks to you!" The player would try again and the old man would pipe up, "For all of us!" Somehow, we made it work. The player was incredibly kind and we all learned something about patience.

On another occasion, in a hot apartment on the north side of Chicago, a player filmed a spot with a woman who had severe physical problems. She could barely control her shaking. She really struggled and so did we as we sweated through the afternoon in her small apartment trying to complete the spot. Finally, she said, "I know what you're thinking. I wish I could stop, but I can't. I'm trapped inside this body." All of us needed to take a deep breath and go outside on the fire escape and cry a little.

My favorite spot was the first one I wrote. We were in Denver and the spot featured one of the Broncos with a beautiful young blind girl. We shot it in Red Rocks Park. She read from a children's book—*The Little Engine That Could*. "Up-up-up the mountain the little engine chugged." It aired for the first time on a Monday night game. I watched it with my wife. She turned to me, "That sounds just like you. Kind of pathetic." We divorced about a year later.

The campaign was a great partnership, not just a convenient relationship. The series lasted for years. The image of the NFL as a league was genuinely enhanced. The spots became an anticipated part of games. They were formulaic but somehow believable. The players wanted to participate. The commissioners, both Pete Rozelle and Paul Tagliabue, cared about the campaign. United Way got invaluable exposure. United Way of America strengthened its position as the national organization vis-à-vis local United Way chapters. Mario's energy and commitment were incredible. I drafted the scripts and took care of pre-production while he directed every spot. He knew the best spots were stories and he always looked for them. The player, for example, whose father would not have been alive without the help he got from a United Way-funded agency.

Writing and helping to produce these football spots was a lot of fun. After the first year United Way asked me to join them as Vice President of Marketing. I said yes, as much as I enjoyed working with Porter Novelli. It probably wasn't a smart "career move" and I really enjoyed working with Novelli but I loved what I was doing..

Besides the football spots, Mario each year conceived and directed a short film for United Way to use during their annual fundraising drives. He managed to convince a number of aging stars to appear. Mickey Rooney, for example, and Elizabeth Taylor. I wrote a film starring Frank Gifford. Leslie Nielsen, when his career was going nowhere, appeared in one of these films. On the set, I asked him what he was up to. He said, "Oh, I'm working on a rather silly film. I don't imagine it will go anywhere." I asked him the name of the film. He said, "Airplane." The rest is history. "Don't call me Shirley."

So there I was a few years out of Harvard Business School writing scripts for football players and Hollywood stars. Every now and then, I'd have lunch with Carrie Rozelle, the commissioner's wife and a United Way board member, to update her on the campaign. She had a prime table at the 21 Club, a Manhattan restaurant and bar frequented by the rich and famous. She was beautiful and smart and usually had an omelet or a salad. I always had a hamburger. You can't take Pittsburgh out of the boy.

I wasn't getting paid much, but I didn't care. I'm sure my classmates were enjoying their careers on Wall Street, but I, in fact, was having a ball. Newly single, I was particularly enjoying the travel and the Washington, D.C. night scene. It was the era of disco and wall-to-wall vodka tonics. On many nights, the Mustang somehow drove its way home. I was living an unsustainable, post-divorce lifestyle. But, believe it or not, I was actually starting to apply some of the basic things I had learned at HBS about marketing.

The marketing function at United Way was pretty feeble. The people were well-intentioned, but their marketing efforts were weak at best. There was no real research. "Why do people give? Because they care. Oh." United Way's message could be summed up in one word: "Give." It delivered that message to all potential donors, rich or poor, old or young. Part of it was habit. The other was a belief that everyone should give to help others in their communities. We started some research to learn more about givers and what motivated them and found, among other things, that there was a strong correlation between relatively large donations and donors' appreciation for the way United Way chapters chose the recipients of their funds. Basically, local volunteers did it through what were called allocation committees.

I suggested to the heads of the larger United Way chapters that they start emphasizing this idea in their fundraising efforts. I didn't get very far. Most of the time I was told that the message was too cerebral and we needed to stick to pictures of destitution and need. So I worked up a poster that had a picture of a young girl next to a picture of an old man. The headline read, "Who do you help first? This girl living with her blindness or this old man dying of his loneliness? That's the question your United Way faces every year. It helps you make that decision." Near as I can tell, this was the first time United Way was going after secondary rather than primary demand, targeting people who had already decided to give.

The message actually tested well, but again no pickup from the locals. In many cases, marketing is limited by an organization's identity. United Way was completely about convincing or coercing people to give, not what to give to and why. But I learned something you will hear about later in this memoir. You can bring emotion into any concept, product or service, even if it's bug spray. The real challenge is to combine thinking and feeling.

We decided in my second year at United Way (1979) to produce some United Way radio ads about a new program called "Service and Referral." It was an effort to let people know about the various organizations that are funded by United Way chapters (they were different in each community) and how to reach them. I decided to approach Himan Brown, who had produced the CBS *Radio Mystery Theater* and before that *Inner Sanctum*, *The Thin Man* and literally thousands of other shows. He was a master. He could use words to create stories that were incredibly compelling. I visited him in New York on 52nd Street and asked him to create 10 radio spots. I gave him examples—typical ones like the Boys & Girls Clubs, and others, such as rehab services and services for families with children who had learning disabilities. He said, "Yes, come back and see me in two weeks." Two weeks later, I came back. I sat down in Himan's office and he turned on a tape recorder. There was a woman's voice. "Yes, this is his mother. Yes, I know his grades have been low. (Pause.) What do you mean he's not like the other students? (She starts to cry.) What do you mean you want to put him into a special school?" You could hear, literally hear, the heartbreak. Voice: "If you need help, call your United Way here in ____. We can find it for you."

Himan proceeded to play the rest of the spots, which he had written and recorded in the two weeks since I met him. There were the voices of Tammy Grimes, E.G. Marshal and other stars he had worked with. He had convinced them all to participate. I took the spots back to United Way with genuine gratitude and excitement and played them for the CEO, a very capable and visionary man. He listened and said, "Bill, these are great. But they are too real. Our people operate at a higher level of misery." Live and learn. The spots did get broadcast in many locations and United Way chapters started getting calls for help, but the "for all of us" message never really was delivered. I'm not sure United Way's people believed it. It wasn't how they thought of themselves.

I did enjoy a few successes. I was asked to develop an effort to promote United Way to school children. Everyone assumed that the message was, you guessed it, give! It wasn't. It was, volunteer! I used the old basics of marketing—product, place, price and promotion—to explain the campaign and people got it. They realized that the "product" of volunteering was the right one for young people.

In various ways, I have stayed involved with the NFL throughout my career. Joe remained a friend and a solid source of advice. Eventually, he took over all the NFL's public relations and reported directly to the commissioner. He introduced me to Dan Rooney, owner of the Steelers. Joe and I had dinner with Dan and his wife Pat in the backyard of their house in Pittsburgh right next to the stadium. I stayed involved with United Way as well. Around 2005, I joined the board of United Way International and chaired it for a few years before we merged it with United Way of America. Joe and I then served on that board for several years.

But back then, in the late '70s, as much as I enjoyed my work at United Way and the Super Bowl tickets I got each year (saw the Steelers win twice), I began to worry that my short career in marketing was limited to not-for-profit experience and I would get labeled as such. Today, a person can bridge the gap between the profit and the non-profit worlds because of the success of social enterprises (more on that later), but not back in 1979.

Then came the call from McKinsey.

3

JOINING
MCKINSEY

WHY WOULD A HEADHUNTER call me to see if I was interested in a position he described as director of marketing at McKinsey? Why would he call me again after I turned him down? Working at United Way's headquarters in Alexandria, Virginia didn't put me in the spotlight of executive recruiters. I certainly wasn't a big-time advertising executive nor was I a public relations pro with an impressive list of clients.

The short answer is McKinsey's headhunter knew Exxon's senior marketing executive. That exec, Ken Kansas, was the volunteer head of United Way's communications committee because the CEO and chairman of Exxon, Cliff Garvin, chaired the United Way board. Ken became my friend and took the time to give me lots of good advice. He also recommended me to the headhunter. That explains call number one. But why, after I told the headhunter about my Mustang convertible and that I wasn't interested, did he call me back about three months later? For that, I need to give you a little more background.

McKinsey had an outstanding reputation. Founded in the mid-'20s, it had assembled a sterling roster of clients. It did not need to market or sell itself. It was word of mouth and relationships. Despite this, in the '70s, McKinsey was challenged by a relatively new firm, the

Boston Consulting Group. BCG had developed some theories about corporate strategy that became well known and admired. They encompassed these theories in what they called the "growth-share matrix." Divisions of companies were classified as either high- or low-growth businesses and they had either high or low share of their markets. Depending on where they were, you either invested in them, milked them or sold them off. BCG started grabbing lots of clients through seminars they held for CEOs and, equally important, getting lots of press. McKinsey started to worry it had lost its luster and that BCG was perceived as smarter consultants. That really stung McKinsey.

To make matters worse, BCG came up with a way to hire the top students out of business schools. They developed an "exploding" offer. They offered students 20 percent more than McKinsey and gave them one week to accept. They could afford to because they didn't have McKinsey's cost structure. So, by the late '70s, BCG's marketing strategy was developing momentum with clients and recruits and becoming a real threat to McKinsey. McKinsey's senior partners decided it needed to develop a marketing strategy too, or at least hire a director of marketing to develop and execute it.

Like other management consultants, they weren't that good at managing themselves so they didn't get around to writing a job description. Maybe they thought that the candidate would figure that out. My guess is they interviewed a lot of marketing pros in New York. That's where McKinsey's "headquarters," such as it existed, was located. The corporate staff was relatively small because the firm was run basically at the office level. At the time, there were about 25 offices worldwide.

McKinsey hired me almost as I walked in the door. I figure between the first and second call from the headhunter they realized that a corporate marketing executive was not going to work for them. Nor would a top newspaper editor or advertising executive. The culture would likely reject people with these backgrounds. Plus, it wasn't clear what was needed. So, they came back to me, the idiot in Washington who turned them down. I even told them that I was not experienced in press relations and not a good editor. Yet, I looked good on paper. Graduated second in my class from Andover. Scholarships to Harvard College. Teacher and stockbroker after that, then Harvard Business School. I don't know if my two jobs in marketing/communications at Porter Novelli and United Way made any difference to them. I doubt that they saw, as I did in retrospect, that what I had been learning about selling ephemeral products like charity and compliance with therapy was, in fact, great training for the job, whatever it was. Consulting is hard to put in a box or otherwise package and its benefits aren't always clear, even if they are real.

So on a frigid night in January, I found myself in a cab on the 59th Street Bridge, not having much of a clue about what was ahead. The Mustang was left behind. So were several girlfriends. It was a new life. What was waiting for me was a sink-or-swim situation. But a friendly sink or swim. The partners wanted help but too often equated help with publishing. The managing partner, Ron Daniel, basically told me to figure out what McKinsey needed and make it happen. I had lots of freedom and the next two years turned out to be two of the most exciting and rewarding years of my life. I learned a tremendous amount about marketing a professional service firm, about building an institutional reputation, the importance of relationships and working hard to really understand the ideas you were trying to promote.

Most of the partners did, in fact, think the biggest part of my job was making sure McKinsey published a lot and looked smart. This was not surprising if you think about the marketing-space—not marketplace—of the group of consultants who aspired to serve big companies on their strategies. There were, to my mind, two dimensions to this space: process and results. The process dimension, call it the x-axis, ranged from well-defined methodologies that were strictly followed to inspired analyses that could change direction several times like a detective looking for clues. The y-axis of the space was about results and what was often called execution.

The method and process consultants delivered a set of recommendations, a "solution." The detective crowd delivered ideas, hypotheses and insights that might lead to, but did not guarantee, a strategic breakthrough. The process/perfection box of this matrix was occupied mainly by the big accounting firms at the time who were trying to break into strategy consulting. The upper right box, call it the exploration/insight box, was dominated by McKinsey, BCG and later Bain.

Revenues per consultant tended to increase dramatically as you moved from lower left to upper right. So did the importance of the relationship with top management. The process guys served the institution. McKinsey and the insight consultants served the CEO. The marketing strategies of the accountants were basically selling their experience. They said, "We did this for this client, followed these approaches and methods, and the results were great."

The marketing message of the insight players was more vague, promising that if you hung around with them, you would discover important ideas and start to think more critically and analytically. They predictably focused their marketing on publication in places like the Harvard Business Review. McKinsey also produced the McKinsey Quarterly, but it wasn't much of a factor in 1980. This was the terrain of management consultants I inherited. Interestingly, I was not asked to run the Quarterly or manage the relationship with HBR, although both would become part of my orbit within a few years.

When I arrived, there was one and only one description of McKinsey. It was about 1,000 words long and chiseled in stone. There was no sizzle in it. McKinsey didn't need to sizzle. The rule was you could send it to a prospective client, but it had to be typed, never copied.

It was a pretty conservative place. The head of McKinsey's office in Los Angeles didn't allow employees to have facial hair. If you left your office, you had to put your jacket on. Until the late '50s, everyone wore hats when they went outside. Consultants wrote prose, careful articulate prose with only a few charts. One old-timer told me he met with his client, the chairman of a major financial institution, every Monday down on Wall Street. On his way back to the office, he wrote a note on yellow paper outlining priorities and carefully discussing the strengths and weaknesses of the top executives. The note went back down by messenger like clockwork. That was it.

Press relations did not exist. Ron told me that if I managed to get one favorable article about McKinsey in a major publication (Fortune, Forbes, etc.) every three or four years, that would be okay. The head of our San Francisco office said he never wanted to see McKinsey's name in the Chronicle. Same with Atlanta, Boston, Dallas and most of the other U.S. cities where we had offices. Outside the U.S., relations varied from cozy to distrustful.

I had no budget, but unlimited airplane tickets—first class airplane tickets. I decided I wasn't going to sit in my office, a drab affair on 46th and Park, and analyze things: marketing expenditures by country or office, for example. Would anyone care? Management consultants do not manage themselves outside of personnel processes that determine compensation and advancement. And I was not a good manager. Team builder, yes, manager, no.

So I started wandering around. Without much planning, I started wandering around in the organization practice.

A word of explanation. Practices at firms such as McKinsey were secondary management mechanisms. Most decisions were made at the geographic or office level. McKinsey put practices in place in the 1970s to develop ideas that might be useful in client work and to publish them. At first, they funded industry practices—basically affinity groups that would gather at nice hotels around the world to discuss what they were learning about the electronics, energy, aerospace and other industries. In the late '70s, Daniel formally funded three functional practices: strategy, organization and operations. The people in these practices were both client-serving consultants who knew something or wanted to know something about the subject and specialists who advised the teams serving clients or did research.

The strategy practice was at the time the big deal. It was going, people hoped, to come up with better ideas than BCG's. That's where the real men (this was the 1970s and it was mostly men), the big thinkers, hung out. The organization practice had a very different personality. Some very capable and successful consultants led it, but it also had a lot of oddballs—people who spent more time thinking and writing than consulting. The strategy practice was pretty dull and quantitative. Is a nine-box matrix really that much better than a four-box matrix? The organization practice was more lively. It looked outside McKinsey as much as inside to find new ideas about what made organizations work. Maybe because I am a bit of an iconoclast and felt like an outsider, I found myself hanging out with the organization practice when they met in San Francisco, Toronto, Paris and other nice places. And that's how I encountered my first great colleague and conspirator at McKinsey, Tom Peters.

I met Tom in the executive washroom at McKinsey's New York office. He seemed to be trying to take a bath in the sink. His suit had clearly been slept in. He said, "Hi, I'm Tom Peters, I just flew in from Frankfurt."

"What were you doing there?"

"I was giving a speech on some research we have been doing on organization performance."

"How did it go?"

"Great!"

Tom was a wild man. He did not fit into McKinsey, but his exuberance and intelligence were undeniable. When I met him in 1980, he was co-authoring a book that would be titled *In Search of Excellence*. We hit it off immediately. He asked me to become a member of the organization practice and help promote the book. I read it and was excited about it. It purported to explain with eight principles what excellent management looked like. Principles like "stick to your knitting" and "do it, try it, fix it." The strategists in McKinsey were not impressed with it. It wasn't sufficiently rigorous for them. And it wasn't great research. But it was perfectly timed.

It was a paean to American management and it came out just when Japan Inc. was being touted as superior to American management. Japanese cars and consumer electronics were dominating our markets. When Lew Young, the editor-in-chief of Business Week saw the research, he asked to meet with Tom and me. He offered to write an article about it. We said yes and before we knew it, a 5,000-word cover story appeared in BW lauding McKinsey and its thinking. The strategists in the firm were jealous and downplayed the article, but that kind of press was pretty impressive. People wanted to hear something good about American management and McKinsey had given it to them.

In the early '80s, business books were not really promoted. If they sold a few thousand copies, they were considered a success. Most were written by professors. But we were onto something. I had become good friends with Adam Meyerson at the Wall Street Journal and Walter Kiechel at Fortune and asked them to review *Excellence*. Tom sent the book to his friend Jim Fallows at the Atlantic. Three positive reviews appeared within two weeks of the publication date. And the rest is history. The book sold millions of copies. It was unprecedented.

Tom, after a few years, left McKinsey and became one of the first of a new breed of management gurus. Not the likes of Peter Drucker or John Gardner. But more Elmer Gantry. He gave speeches that were zealous and entertaining. Some of Tom's partners complained that the book, which McKinsey paid for, did more for Tom than McKinsey, but that was quibbling.

I liked the organization practice because I understood its ideas and its members were friendly and fun-loving. Its concepts were more inductive than deductive and certainly not rigorous. But they didn't need to be. They needed to be useful to a good consultant. For example, one of the practice's most basic concepts was that organizations should be analyzed along seven parameters. To help people remember all seven, they drew seven bubbles in a circle connected by lines and named each of the elements so it started with "s." Shared values, skills, systems, superordinate goal, etc. And then they said, to make your company perform better, Mr. CEO, you've got to get all the s's aligned or "roughly headed west." That was it. No fancy analytics, very few numbers, but enough of a framework to support a succession of consulting assignments. Not for nothing did the practice call this picture the "happy atom." It brought in a lot of revenues and underscored the thought that it was better to be roughly right than precisely wrong.

Tom and his co-author Bob Waterman gave me a lot of credit for helping them and the organization practice. As a result, the strategy practice asked me to work with them and I, of course, did. Fred Gluck, who would succeed Ron Daniel as managing partner, ran the strategy practice. He knew what he wanted to do. He did not want to publish one big idea on strategy to defeat BCG. He wanted to develop all kinds of ideas and get the partners to try them out and share the results. He put together a one-week seminar on strategy that all partners were expected to attend. Once every two or three months, I would go to these seminars in Vevey, Switzerland and get to know partners from around the world. What an opportunity. And what fun. Let's just say, what happened in Vevey stayed in Vevey.

Fred's mission was to instill a love for ideas in the firm. I remember once he came into my office yelling, "Look at this!" It was a presentation that argued that if a company wanted to turn itself around, the CEO needed to be canned. I said to Fred that our client CEOs might not welcome that thinking. He didn't care. He didn't care about the politics. And he didn't care if an idea generated a lot of revenue. If it got used just once, that was fine with him. Not all the partners agreed. I got to help Fred do what he wanted to do and he succeeded. Eventually, he asked me to invent and put in place systems to spread new ideas around McKinsey. "Get people to talk to each other," he said. "Don't make this a paper exercise." Was all this marketing? Yes, because we were changing the way McKinsey thought about itself and how it worked. That's the essence of marketing in a professional firm.

Looking back, within those first few years I had formed, as Jon Katzenbach, one of the senior partners, used to say, my "own little McKinsey." It was made up of 20 to 30 colleagues and friends who were thought leaders and risk takers. People like Ken Ohmae, for example, the head of McKinsey's office in Japan. One morning, he walked into my office and said, "I am angry!" I asked why. He said, "Because my book is much better than *Excellence.*" He had, in fact, written a good book on strategy. I told him a book on strategy has a much more limited audience. He asked me what he should write about. We agreed he would write about Japan and trade. Was Japan as good as it seemed to be? Were its markets really protected?

Two weeks later, Ohmae walked into my office again and said he could prove Japan consumes more American goods than vice versa.

I said, "I doubt that."

He said, "Here are the numbers."

He was right.

Ken added what Japan imported from the U.S. to what American companies produced in Japan, discounting the latter figure by 50 percent because of ownership limitations Japan imposed on U.S investments. He divided that number by the Japanese population. He did the same thing for the U.S.

Guess what? On a per capita basis, Japan consumed more American goods than Americans consumed Japanese goods, despite all those Japanese cars and cameras. This fact had major policy implications. I sent it to the editorial page of the Wall Street Journal. A few days later, they published Ken's analysis at the top of the page.

I got a lot of phone calls. One from a partner serving a big American electronics firm. Its CEO was not happy with Ohmae's editorial and wondered why McKinsey was "taking Japan's side in the trade debate." I told the partner, whom I knew well because of the seminars in Vevey, we shouldn't restrict what our partners had to say and that Ken was speaking for himself.

I said that if he had another point of view supported by numbers, we could try to publish it. I didn't hear from him.

Another call came from the ambassador to Japan, Mike Mansfield. He asked if the numbers were correct. I said yes. He asked, "What was the name of your partner in Japan?" I said, "Ohmae." He said, "No, oh my God."

Ohmae and I worked together often. I would spend a week or so in Japan every few months. We had a good time running around the Ginza. Ken had a four-box matrix for it: low cost/high cost; low touch/ high touch. He wrote dozens of editorials for the Journal. One night, after dinner at the Four Seasons in New York, Bob Bartley, the editor of the editorial page, asked him to be a contributing editor for the Asian edition. From Tokyo, I branched out to Sydney and Melbourne where McKinsey had very good thinkers. One was John Stuckey, who was beginning to develop some solid ideas about corporate strategy. Another was Clem Dougherty, who knew the best Australian wines well before they were discovered.

Back in New York, I started working closely with several other partners. John Sawhill was one of them. He was head of the energy practice. Sawhill was a former deputy secretary of energy. He wrote several pieces about energy policy for the Journal including one that questioned the wisdom of policies that support integrated oil companies. It too appeared at the top of the Journal's editorial page. Several partners from the energy practice called me and voiced concern, wondering what our clients would think. We found out. Within a few weeks, Sawhill was invited to speak to the boards of just about every integrated oil company.

John was driven by a need to serve his country as well as his clients. He trusted me. He asked me to visit the CEOs of McKinsey's energy clients to ascertain the quality and strength of our relationships. That included Enron. I would meet with John very early in the morning to discuss his thinking. I often found him eating cereal with fruit juice. He had diabetes and died way too young.

I also worked closely with a partner named Lowell Bryan. He wrote a book titled *Breaking up the Bank*. I helped Lowell, who became a good friend, get published in several important newspapers and magazines on the dangers of large integrated banks. Same story, same impact. Like Sawhill, Lowell was determined to make his industry better. He was a tenacious competitor. He almost played pro football. Whenever he lost a negotiation, he persevered to win the relationship back.

My strategy—well, let's call it a rough plan—was to find a few smart, well-intentioned partners and gain attention for their ideas and intentions. Partners such as John and Lowell made that strategy work.

There were others, but not many, because the partners, in general, liked being behind the scenes and not out front. And that was good. But I worked with partners who were willing to take on important issues and publicly own them. They took care to be on solid ground with their analyses. We positioned them as individual partners of McKinsey, not practice leaders speaking for McKinsey. The important point is that together their voices added up to a voice for McKinsey that stood for an independence of thought, a fact-based point of view and an international perspective. It was very different from inventing and publishing some intellectual supernova or a new management acronym.

I wasn't surprised when, in 1982, Fortune published a cover story titled "Corporate Strategists Under Fire." It was written by my good friend Walter Kiechel. It basically said that the recent theories about corporate strategy were overrated and that BCG's strategy matrix was too predictable and blunt. It highlighted a number of other ideas on innovation and growth, including some of McKinsey's. In the middle of the article was a picture of a boxing ring. In the ring were all the strategy consultants—Bain, BCG, Booz, etc. In the middle of the ring, twice as large as the other boxers, was McKinsey. The copy read, "McKinsey has come roaring back—pushing to develop new ideas, hiring strong people, building on what its competitors view as its unassailable asset, the strength of its long-standing relationships with clients."

My colleagues were very happy. They felt we had vanquished our competitors, in particular BCG. They asked for framed copies of the boxing ring illustration. McKinsey was back, once again the "preeminent" management consultant.

Yet, there was something wrong. If you read the article, you got the sense that management consultants were not highly regarded professionals. They were several rungs down from doctors and lawyers. Even dentists were ranked higher. As Fortune writer Walter Guzzardi had said decades earlier, "Management consultants borrowed your watch to tell you the time."

I stopped by to see Ron and asked, "Did you really read the article?"

"Yes, it was fine."

"But," I said, "it wasn't. That ring of consultants was a ring of thugs. We are the biggest thug in that ring."

Ron gave me a look I think he reserved for young partners (I had been elected a partner at this point) and said, "Okay, what do you propose we do?"

I said, "We have to get out of the ring."

He asked, "And just how are we going to do that?'

"I don't know. It's a mystery."

4

CREATING
THE LEADERSHIP
FACTORY

MCKINSEY, at least the senior partners who hired me, wanted me to succeed. The leaders were tough, demanding, widely capable men who had very high standards of performance. I still have, forty years after joining the firm, bad dreams about not being up to the challenge they wanted me to define and meet. It was a place that could be very supportive and then crush you in the next moment. I remember early on being asked to organize and host a weekend event for its retired senior partners. It was a mixed crowd–about 25 of them who came with their wives to have good dinners and listen to presentations about how the firm was growing and the quality of our work and people. Some of them were true founders from the '40s and '50s, for the most part modest men who invented McKinsey under Marvin Bower's guidance. Others had been stars, in the '60s and later, made senior partner and gone off to be CEOs.

So there I was on a Friday morning welcoming them, going over the agenda, trying to be both informative and clever, and wondering to myself what are they thinking about this young guy wearing a bow tie, sporting a mustache and explaining to them that I was the new guy responsible for McKinsey's reputation. I was scared. I was sweating.

In the front row was the CEO of Pepsico. Andy Pearson. Fortune had just written an article that named Andy one of America's "ten toughest bosses." Andy seemed to be staring at me intently as I stumbled through my opening remarks. But as I passed in front of him he touched my sleeve and whispered, "Take it easy. You're doing just fine." It made a big difference. I relaxed and the meeting went well. That was McKinsey. An enigmatic place that loved you and threatened you and demanded excellence.

One Saturday morning, about two years after I joined McKinsey, I got a phone call from a man named Warren Cannon. He was the head of staff. Even though I reported to Ron Daniel, Warren was the guy I went to initially for advice. He was tough and very smart and he seemed to like me.

"Bill, this is Warren."

"Hi," I said, wondering what could be important enough for Warren to call me on a weekend.

"I just wanted you to know you have been elected to the partnership of the firm."

I was genuinely surprised. When I was approached by McKinsey, there was something said about my job being a partnership position and that it could happen as quickly as two years, but I had not broached the subject with anyone and no one had said anything to me.

I thanked Warren and said I knew he was the one who spearheaded my nomination. I didn't know, but figured he did.

"You have created quite a following. Lots of people had good things to say about you. Congratulations."

I thanked him again and hung up. I sat there on an old wooden church pew I had bought from an antique shop in Connecticut, part of the decor in my barn-like loft on 38th and 6th. I thought to myself, not bad. From United Way football spots to partner at McKinsey in two years.

But there were ups and downs. Shortly after getting elected, I discovered I had a brain tumor. It was large, painful, but likely benign. It had to come out. In the morning, after nine hours of surgery, I awakened to find Fred Gluck at the foot of my bed. Shortly after, Ron Daniel joined us. Warren Cannon spent the entire nine hours with my family in the waiting room. Ron sent a note to the firm saying I was fine and "alert." That was code for "he can still think." Fred started introducing me as the McKinsey partner who had his brain removed. That's when you know you belong, and I belonged at McKinsey.

How did this happen? Consider the following thoughts to be conjecture, but here's my answer.

First, I got my personal strategy roughly right. Don't hang around headquarters and lecture the partners about marketing—what little I knew. Pick a few of them to work with and make good things, new things, happen. I went out and embraced McKinsey and it hugged me back. Later I realized this was the right way to change the institutional image of a dispersed, international service firm—one person at a time. Remember the number theory where if you prove something is true for n and n plus 1, then it must be true for n plus 2? Moreover, I really did have a group of partners, many of them leaders of the firm, who trusted me and invited me to dinner at their homes in Paris, London, Tokyo, Frankfurt, Zürich, you name it.

Second, good things were ready to happen when I got there. The firm's leaders had invested heavily in building McKinsey's practices and intellectual capital. I showed up around harvest time. By luck, or foresight, I saw my role as pushing us away from academic theory toward issues that were important to senior managers. McKinsey certainly provided me with the ammunition to do that.

Third, BCG had scared McKinsey. BCG had good clients and good people around the world in countries where we thought we were dominant. Many of the partners felt a need for real change, not just more processes and frameworks.

Fourth, I fit the culture. I had the right educational background. I was in many ways naïve and I came from a poor background. Believe it or not, McKinsey in the early '80s was led by partners who fit that profile. Fred Gluck grew up in a two-and-a-half-room apartment in Brooklyn with five brothers and sisters. His dad was a traveling salesman. In some ways, McKinsey people were superbly capable and, in other ways, not very savvy. That included me. Once, Ohmae and I were in Paris together when Leslie Stahl's people called me. They wanted Ken to debate Boone Pickens, who was complaining that he was being prevented from sitting on boards in Japan. Ken said sure. I said sure. Pickens dominated the debate. It was very frustrating. But we got over it; failure was well tolerated at McKinsey.

Fifth, I didn't fit the culture. I was not a good consultant or manager. I thought business was dull. I saw my role from the outside in, as a good marketer should, and tried to keep my partners honest about the quality of their thinking. I remember once Fred insisted that McKinsey had developed the idea of purchasing power parity. The next morning, I placed a couple of articles on his desk that proved him wrong. My network outside McKinsey became as strong as the one inside. People like Adam Meyerson, Tim Ferguson, David Asman, Dan Henninger and Melanie Kirkpatrick at the Journal, Christopher Lorenz at the Financial Times, Steve Prokesch at Business Week, Steve Lohr at the New York Times and senior people at the Economist. I never asked them for favors and never sent them mediocre thinking. This network included my old friend Joe Browne, who had become an SVP at the NFL and Bruce Nelson, who would become vice chairman at Omnicom—two solid sources of advice on public relations and advertising.

Sixth, I really worked hard to understand the substance of McKinsey's thinking and work even though I wasn't advising clients. Early on, one of the senior partners, Carter Bales, gave me some good advice. He told me to read the 16 staff papers that summarized most of McKinsey's thinking at the time about strategy and organization. I read them all carefully. I did the math. In fact, at Andover I won the math prize. I almost flunked accounting at HBS, but my quantitative skills held me up. I also read external material that I thought we needed to know. I dragged a copy of Robert Solomon's book on the international monetary system to Cape Cod one summer and read it twice. Too many marketers, I suspect, don't really get into the substance of what their companies do and how they deliver value.

Last, and certainly most importantly, Marvin Bower, McKinsey's venerable founder, became my mentor. The first thing I did when I joined McKinsey was read Bower's book *Perspective on McKinsey*. It was daunting. It made me think I was not good enough for McKinsey. In it, Bower explained why he wanted to create a management consulting firm that was as professional as a law firm. It was Bower who turned the firm around in the mid-'30s when James O. McKinsey died. It was Bower who, when he officially took over as managing partner in 1952, hired the first MBAs as consultants, believing that we would deliver more value with brains than experience. It was Bower who refused to fly first class. And most importantly, it was Marvin who insisted that McKinsey be a meritocracy.

We had a nice informal relationship. His office was close to mine. He had retired from active leadership of the firm and would wander in or I would go see him, sometimes on a specific topic or just as often to talk about the firm in general. McKinsey had hired an oral historian to interview at length some of the early senior partners who were getting pretty old. Marvin was one. I was asked to take over this project, both to guard it and use it appropriately. I read Marvin's interview, which covered a couple hundred pages, carefully. So, we had things to talk about. He wasn't in any way ostentatious and not much for entertaining, but I was a regular at his birthday parties.

I became genuinely fond of Marvin and felt that it was a privilege to work with him. He told me he had never seen an outsider understand McKinsey as quickly as I did. But he helped. He asked me not to use the words marketing and brand, and speak more about our reputation and relationship building. I followed his values and principles, and used them to guide what I was trying to do. I worked with senior people as well as junior people, regardless of their status, who had ideas and were well-intentioned. I put the interests of my external network ahead of ours, just as Marvin taught our consultants to do with their clients. Marvin policed McKinsey's vocabulary and I tried to do the same thing. I didn't let people talk about "solutions" or use acronyms to label their thinking. I took my role as keeper of the firm's policies seriously. I reminded our teams they were never to mention client names. Nor were our clients allowed to mention us. These were important rules and I tried to make sure there was zero tolerance for any breaches.

Marvin kept my feet on the ground. I remember once I tried to write a policy on speaking engagements and when we should accept them. Kind of a bad idea to begin with. Sometimes common sense is better than a policy. In any case, I wrote a policy that basically said make sure the speaking opportunity is worth your time and McKinsey's. I asked Marvin to look at it. He did and then he handed it back to me. He said, in a voice that got high and squeaky as he approached 80, "Bill this is fine. You make several good points, but maybe you should start by saying that when someone here is deciding to accept a speaking engagement, he should first ask himself if he has anything worthwhile to say." Yes, I felt pretty stupid.

CREATING THE LEADERSHIP FACTORY

I learned a lot from Marvin and he helped me become a good partner. Sometime in his 80s, I think, Marvin lost his wife of many years, Helen. Not long after, he married a good friend of theirs who lived near them in Bronxville. His new wife Cleo and he bought a place in Florida and started spending time there. Then she died and Marvin was all alone. He started working on a book and would send me chapters. I read them and worried. His previous books were rigorous and structured. But I could find no structure or purpose in what he was now writing. Nevertheless, I kept reading the chapters and their iterations, hoping that they would eventually add up. But they didn't. Finally, he sent me the whole book and asked for a full assessment. This was not something I could do over the phone. I flew down to see him. He met me and we had dinner. Then he walked me back to a guest room in the facility where he was then living. I sat down on the small bed and he on a chair and I told him I did not think he should publish his book, that it wasn't up to his standards. I also told him he could submit it to Harvard Press and they would probably publish it because he was the author. He thanked me. The next morning, we had breakfast before I flew back to New York. We did not talk about the book and he never brought it up again. Some days, I think I did what was best for him; other days, I fear that I let my friend down.

So, the main reason I said to Ron Daniel that we should not be content being the biggest thug in a ring of thugs was Marvin. He wanted to create a profession of management consulting, a respected profession. Even though the Fortune article made the partners feel good, it wasn't good enough. We needed to change McKinsey's aspiration to be the "preeminent strategy consultant." Michael Porter said many smart things, but maybe the smartest was, "Don't aspire to be the best or the biggest; aspire to be unique."

I followed my usual plan, wandering and wondering around, asking the partners, now my partners, what makes McKinsey unique. Almost all the answers were the same: "McKinsey is the preeminent strategy consultant." Tom Peters agreed that it was the right question, but didn't have an answer. However, Carter Bales did. Carter was a senior partner in the New York office. Among other things, he led McKinsey's recruiting efforts at business schools. When I asked Carter my question, he said, "That's easy. We are a leadership factory."

"We are a what?"

"A leadership factory. We produce leaders. We produce more CEOs than any other institution."

Could this be true? I should have known that it might be. In my desk, I kept a handwritten list of all the McKinsey "alumni" who had left and become CEOs of major companies. Reporters were always asking for it. Sometimes I gave it to them, but I never typed it up. Call it preserving the mystique. The list got longer and longer. But what about this dimension of leadership? Did it make sense? Could it be a differentiating factor? More importantly, could it actually change the market-space we were in? I thought it could be much more than a product-market attribute. So did Carter and several others. It had the benefit of being true. We did produce lots of CEOs. And Marvin always insisted that when we consulted we served the CEO and not one of his division heads. That we took what he called an "integrated top-management perspective." On the other hand, Bain and BCG tended to serve companies and even industries. So, was McKinsey essentially an elite group of future leaders serving leaders?

It seems obvious, doesn't it? That leadership was part of McKinsey's identity and value? But sometimes you are too close to see it or articulate it. Yes, we knew we were doing more than saving our clients' money and helping them redirect their strategies. But more important, we were supporting and advancing the quality of leadership in the corporate sector both in the U.S. and other prospering economies. We needed to think about that idea and live up to it.

4

Once we discovered, or rediscovered, our strength, we needed to do something about it. In fact, we did three things. First, Carter and I changed McKinsey's standard recruiting pitch. When we went to campus, Carter made it very clear that no one was to talk about making partner. That happened for only one in eight people who joined McKinsey and it took several years. Instead, we talked about joining McKinsey to finish off your preparation to lead companies. BCG and Bain and other strategy consultants couldn't say that. They didn't have our history or orientation.

Second, we beefed up our placement capabilities. I had been asked to run alumni relations when I arrived, but I did not do much. In general, people were treated well when they left McKinsey so we made modest efforts to stay in touch with them and help them stay in touch with each other. But we began to make improvements in our systems so that when people left, they had several job offers rather than one or two. In general, the positions they were offered were in senior management ranks.

Third, I continued to raise the bar on our external communications. While we still published articles about management in the Harvard Business Review, we focused more of our attention on issues that were affected by policy and international competition. In addition to Ohmae, Sawhill and Bryan, other practice leaders and individuals joined our efforts to own issues. On the other hand, we basically gave away our management ideas rather than treat them as if they were secret formulae. What, after all, do consultants offer? Three things: people, skills and knowledge. McKinsey did not offer solve-the-problem methodologies as our competitors did. Instead, our editorials on issues that mattered to senior management positioned us as leaders, not consultants.

The repositioning was valuable to us in several ways. Students now saw McKinsey as a next step rather than the end point in their careers.

They did not need to make partner to succeed. If it happened, it happened. Clients saw our young consultants as leaders in waiting and were more willing to pay for their time. And institutions, semi-public and public, not well known to us made overtures of various kinds because they saw us as an influential network. Eventually, we formed the McKinsey Global Institute. Its work, which married macro- and micro-economic analysis, greatly enhanced and extended McKinsey's reputation. It was a powerful change in our identity, this new dimension. We were seen differently and we saw ourselves differently.

I describe all this many years after it occurred. Hindsight is an exact science. I'm sure we did not put these efforts on paper as a tripartite plan. But they did fit together. Two years after the cover story in Fortune that featured McKinsey in the boxing ring, another cover story about us appeared. Its headline was, "Who Produces the Most CEOs, GE or McKinsey?" I don't remember who won. And it didn't matter. This time, McKinsey was in the ranks of the world's most admired companies: GE, IBM, 3M, P&G, etc. We had jumped out of the ring of thugs.

Was Marvin pleased? Had Carter and I, and the others who helped execute our plan, effectively told the world McKinsey was a unique professional institution? I think so. I hope so. Professions start and end with the quality of the people in their ranks. We had positioned McKinsey as an organization that starts and ends with leaders.

I want to pick up two points later in this memoir. First, the market-space is malleable. You can change it dramatically by reconceiving its dimensions. Sure, consulting is about process and results, but it can be about other things too—other things that not only differentiate and put you at the top of the pack, but put you into a whole new pack. Good marketers think hard and creatively about what those dimensions might be and how they can use them to bend the space and to bend it to their advantage.

Second, to actually change the perspective and position of your firm, whether you consult or make soda pop, you probably need to do three or four things that somehow add up to a coordinated and sustained effort. Doing just one thing probably won't be enough. McKinsey needed to do more than change its recruiting pitch. But doing several things isn't going to work either. You see many companies today try to change their image by adopting a new theme of the week: sustainability, diversity, convenience, nutrition, opulence, organic. Don't be a chameleon. Identify new dimensions of value and then do things to substantiate your claim to be uniquely good in the new space you have defined.

You may, or may not, change your business model or adopt new technologies. But you need to see yourself in a substantially different way. History teaches us there were two messages at the entrance to the Oracle at Delphi. Honor the Stranger. And First Know Thyself.

5

CLOTHES MAKE
THE MAN

You load sixteen tons, what do you get
Another day older and deeper in debt
Saint Peter don't you call me 'cause I can't go
I owe my soul to the company store.

Sixteen Tons—Tennessee Ernie Ford

i SHOULD BACK UP BRIEFLY and explain a little more of my past. In 1962 I went off to Andover. Twenty years later I was elected a partner at McKinsey. I had taught English literature, coached soccer, sold stocks and bonds, earned an MBA, and learned a little about selling ephemeral things like compliance and charity. Now, in 1985, I was getting my suits tailored.

In London when you get a bespoke suit, you don't take it with you after the final fitting, Your tailor, a Mr. Arrington in my case, carries it from his little shop on Sackville Street to your hotel and leaves it for you. And so it was for me. Over the years he brought at least 10 suits, a top coat and a couple of tuxedos. The suit was modeled on one that my Harvard roommate had made for him. A one-button jacket of 9-10 ounce gaberdine, solid back, broad rounded shoulders and peak lapels, not too wide. The trousers had a single, inverted pleat, a button fly, British back so the suspenders fit right, and a 1 and a quarter inch cuff. It all looked pretty good with a bow tie. (See picture of me with Marvin Bower later in the book.)

My partners noticed. McKinsey consultants dressed conservatively. They wore boxy woolen suits. Very American even outside the States. Warren Cannon said the style reminded him of "moderately well-to-do morticians." When they were outside their offices, they always wore hats until Marvin stopped wearing one sometime in the '60s. No one knows why.

I was spending a lot of time in London because by the middle of the '80s I had become responsible for publishing the McKinsey Quarterly and it was based there. I saw no reason to move its operations. I liked London–the plays on the West End, the parks, the culture, even the food. I liked the other cities in McKinsey's network and spent a lot of time on planes traveling internationally. McKinsey did things first class and that included air travel and good hotels.

New York City, however, remained home for me. After getting elected a partner I purchased a new apartment–a loft on 29th street on the West side in Chelsea. The neighborhood was a little sketchy. Some of my colleagues were afraid to visit when their black cars brought them down from the Upper East Side. But the place was great! It was a whole floor. The elevator opened onto almost 3,000 square feet. There were large windows everywhere, two terraces and a greenhouse. I filled it with trees and plants. My social life was busy. There was an uptown, McKinsey side of it and a downtown Soho side of it. I dated lots of women, one quite seriously for almost 10 years. Like me she was a double Harvard. She was beautiful and smart and kind. But we were incompatible. She must have moved in and out five times.

I started buying some art, but I was pretty careful about money. The coal miner was still in me. Pay in cash and don't take on any debt. With my bonuses I paid off the new place in a few years. There may have been times when I should have carried some debt, but if you grow up poor, you think poor; poor is always just around the corner. And you feel second class. At least I did, below the surface. Most of these feelings dissipated at McKinsey as I continued to do well and make more money than I ever thought I would make. But because I was not actually consulting McKinsey clients I sometimes felt insecure. Maybe all McKinsey partners felt this way. Ron Daniel used to say we were a bunch of "insecure overachievers."

Andover had left its marks on me, not all of them good. I felt very poor and very lower class when I was there. I had to work in the dining hall because I was on scholarship and that didn't help. I had one sports jacket, one tie and a few acceptable shirts—none made in London. On the soccer field I had to wear used cleats while the others wore shiny new Adidas and Pumas. I could feel the condescension from some of my classmates. Some resented me because I studied so hard and they didn't or they were not very smart. They had been born wealthy and privileged but not intelligent. Nevertheless they could stop by the Andover Shop and buy several silk ties at once and a few perfect blazers, grey wool trousers and penny loafers. Those damn penny loafers. They had the right uniform. I spent two years at Andover, graduated second in my class and got three full scholarships to Harvard. And all the time I was there I was miserable and lonely.

Some days were especially tough. There were no girls at Andover. For spring prom you had to import them from schools such as Dana Hall if you weren't lucky enough to know one from nearby Abbot Academy. I didn't. The only girls I knew were back in western Pennsylvania. And they didn't have the bus fare. So on prom night I stood by myself watching vans and cars pull up to deposit pretty girls in gowns who were greeted by my well dressed classmates. It didn't help when I told myself I was a much better dancer than any of them. I walked back to my dormitory feeling sorry for myself. But the next morning I got up and vowed "Never again."

My good friend Bill Novelli grew up as I did in a town full of immigrants. "We were all very poor," he once said to me, "but we didn't know it."

Andover let me know it. And maybe Indianola did too. People would "give you the shirt off their back" but they would also call you names to make themselves feel that they belonged and you didn't. I got called some pretty mean names, even by my friends. It hurt. It was as if they didn't want others to get ahead. When I won the scholarships a rumor spread around town that my mother understated our income. She could have tripled it and it wouldn't have made any difference. My mother was determined to get me out of Indianola. She almost chained me to a street car, dragging me into Pittsburgh to take secondary school admissions tests. I guess I did well because Andover sent me a letter, Exeter a postcard. Each offered full tuition of $1,800. I picked Andover.

My mother was remarkable. She would do anything for her children, even send them away. Our neighbors didn't understand how she could do that. She made the world brighter. On Halloween our house was the most visited. She handed out popcorn balls. And she made everyone sign a "guest book." Not trick or treaters, but guests. She did this year after year. Older brothers and sisters would bring their younger siblings by and show them where they had signed years earlier. Parents too.

My mother loved to dance, especially the polka, and was first on the dance floor at weddings, often dragging me with her.

Then, in late summer of 1962 it was time for me to leave. We all went down to the Greyhound bus terminal in Pittsburgh. I said goodbye to my brother and sister and my father. Then I looked at my mother and quickly turned away and got on the bus. I knew and she knew we would start to cry if we embraced.

Sadly, foolishly, for many years I was ashamed of my mother. She wasn't, I feared, classy enough, for my new standard of living. I took her to Rome, Amsterdam, London and several American cities, but I was always afraid she would somehow embarrass me. Did Andover and Harvard do that to me? Or was I just stupid? Over lunch when I was about 50, my friend Larry Ackerman, who really understood corporate identity, asked me what in my life I regretted most. I told him that I regretted that I made my mother feel inferior or behaved impatiently with her. Larry told me to write her a letter and tell her I was sorry and regretted what I had done. And I did. She told me it was okay. It was part of a bargain she had understood and anticipated. She was always way ahead of me. Thank goodness.

There was a hill near our house overlooking the mine. I used to go there, lie on the grass and watch the trains come in to pick up the coal. The locomotives were powered by steam and sent big white clouds into the sky. Three or four of them would come in during the day. Then it was just one, a diesel. The coal was running out. Houses were beginning to sink. The steel industry was beginning to move offshore. By the time I left for Andover, the mine, the doctor's office, the company store were all gone. Even the tracks were torn up.

There was a creek that ran through the middle of town. We all swam in it. It was beautiful. It had rapids and deep holes and smooth rocks for sunbathing. One day, all of a sudden, its green waters became an ugly yellow-brown. A plant upstream started to dump sulphur-filled waste into it. No one asked. No one complained. We kept swimming in it. We had nowhere else to go.

My studies at Harvard College included no courses on political science or economics. All you had to do to graduate was pass one course in the physical sciences, one in social sciences and one in humanities. Then you could just bounce around and study whatever you wanted. So my course work didn't help me form a point of view about how society should work. The idea that capital and labor somehow got mixed together to produce "progress" and wealth was not on my learning agenda.

But, in fact, I had seen the struggle between capital and labor when I was growing up. My little town was created and dominated by capital. Sometime in the '20s, Republic Steel laid out the streets and built every house. The inhabitants were segregated by nationality and race. The Polish lived in one section, the Italians in another. A mix of eastern Europeans lived on a hill called "Peanut Heaven." African-Americans lived just across the street from my grandmother.

Everyone was poor. And everyone worked for Republic. My dad was 14 when he went into the mine for the first time. He was smart and reportedly skipped two grades of school. His reward was a forged birth certificate and a job. Like his father he became an alcoholic. He died when he was 53. He was mean when he was drunk. He would stumble home and box us around. When he was about 50 he was told another drink would kill him. So he stopped drinking. I felt sorry for him because I think he realized at the end that he could have been so much more than he was. I don't think he had much of a chance to defeat the forces around him. He actually attended my graduation from Harvard College. It was the first graduation in Harvard's history to be rained out. Because I was a class marshal, I was able to take him and my mom to the ceremonies in Sanders Theater. I could see the wonder in his eyes. He was proud of me.

My father became a boss in the mine so he did not go underground that often. He never wanted us to see it. Because he was in management, he could not join the union. When the mine closed he got nothing. The miners got pensions. My mother filed for and got black lung benefits when he died. I told her he didn't deserve them. That dad died from liver disease. She replied that I wasn't learning much at Harvard and that she needed the money.

Tennessee Ernie Ford sang a song with the refrain "I owe my soul to the company store." That was Indianola. A family's debt at the store was deducted from each month's paycheck. Most of what was left was spent at The Rod and Gun Club on whiskey and beer. My mother cleaned houses for six dollars a day. I delivered newspapers. She helped me on cold mornings. I carried them up and down the hills, or used a wagon on Sundays, or a sled. I made about twenty dollars a month and she got fifteen of that. She needed and deserved it.

It took me years to understand that being a partner of McKinsey meant that I was an owner. Literally an owner. Fred Gluck drummed it into my head. "Think like an owner," he would say. For me democracy and capitalism did not have much to do with ownership. You worked for the man and he didn't care about you. But it was worse in other places. Indianola in the '40s and '50s when I was growing up was relatively benign compared to other towns and times when real class warfare existed. If you want to know more, not about me but how this country struggled to survive, read *Playing Through the Whistle: Steel, Football, and an American Town*. It's about Aliquippa, a steel town west of Indianola, a bigger, tougher, meaner town that was owned and run by Jones and Laughlin Steel Company. The accounts in the book of what life was like are remarkable. People who think America hasn't come a long way in terms of the health and happiness of an average citizen see a different country than I do. That's not to say social and economic progress was smooth. We almost lost the steel industry in America because of the battles between capital and labor and the economics that pushed production to Japan and elsewhere.

And yet here I am, a coal miner's son in well cut suits, who believes, not without doubt, that we can make this country even greater than it already is. That somehow we can harness the tremendous talents and values of our citizens, new and old, and that marketing, albeit redefined, can create tremendous new wealth and bring stakeholders together. That marketing can be a powerful force for progress in other countries as well. That said, maybe it's time to get back to my story.

6

NEW
DIMENSIONS

MY WIFE, PAMELA, AND I own a house designed by Philip Johnson. Johnson was the most prominent of a group of architects who developed "mid-century modern" design. They were called the Harvard Five–Johnson, Marcel Breuer, Landis Gores, John Johansen and Eliot Noyes. All of them settled in and around New Canaan, Connecticut or spent weekends there. The houses they built were controversial and not always well received. There were no curves, only corners, open spaces and flat roofs. Sometime in the mid-'40s, Johnson was challenged by his mentor, Ludwig Mies van der Rohe, to build a house of glass. He did in 1948-'49 and that house, the Glass House, is one of the most famous houses in America.

In the early '50s, a wealthy French family asked Johnson to design a house for them. It would eventually become ours. According to Johnson, they said, "We like your little house of glass, but we want a glass villa. We are European and we have a family." Johnson, on one of several visits he made to our house, told us he wasn't initially sure he could do that. But then, he said, he figured it out. He laid the house out on a grid of 16-foot squares defined by steel and brick pillars. Five squares wide and eight squares long. Some of these squares were "inside," some outside on brick terraces, and some on grass that extended to the end of the grid. What Johnson did was effectively redefine what was inside and out. In the original Glass House, the glass itself demarcated what was in and out. In ours, with its 12 tons of glass, the boundaries were the pillars that extended beyond the living spaces. "You realize," he once remarked to us, "that I was breaking up the Miesien cube when I built your house." We laughed. "Of course!"

So, several years after Johnson defined a new space for architecture with his Glass House, he was redesigning it again with ours. I suspect that this is what great marketers do. They literally see new dimensions for how value is measured and pricing is set. They figure out where in the new space they want their products and services to be. They are conceptual architects. And in many ways, they are also rebels. They are not content with adjustments. I can't prove this, of course, and goodness knows marketing would not survive without product extensions that are improvements along existing dimensions. But I can give you some examples of game changers who insisted on seeing the world differently.

One of them was Rawleigh Warner. Rawleigh was the chairman of Mobil Oil. He did not fit the profile of the heads of major oil companies. He was a finance guy rather than an engineer. He went to Wharton. He spent very little time in the oil patch. Rawleigh headed Mobil when big oil was, if not reviled, certainly distrusted. Rawleigh and his wife Mary Ann lived close by in New Canaan. We met them because their house was designed by John Johansen, another member of the Harvard Five. The Warners had a wonderful house built over a stream. Lots of glass, impressive art. (We all should have a Motherwell over the fireplace.) Rawleigh and I were also connected because McKinsey had served Mobil extensively when he was running things. He thought very highly of Ron Daniel, who headed the relationship for McKinsey.

Rawleigh mentioned a couple of things about marketing and design that intrigued me, so one Saturday morning we got together at his place to talk, over the stream and under the Motherwell. Early in the conversation, he said that when he took over he wanted to humanize Mobil. People, the people who buy gas, saw it as a big, powerful, international company with little regard for the masses. That didn't sit well with him and it didn't sit well with Mary Ann. So they did three things.

First, they hired Eliot Noyes (another member of the Harvard Five) to redesign Mobil's gas stations. In essence, Noyes put big umbrellas over the pumps. The first stations appeared in South America. "You get out of the car and it's hot. You're pumping gas; you need some shade," he said. The reaction was very positive and soon Mobil was redefining what gas stations looked like all over the world. Second, Mobil started to sponsor a television series entitled *Masterpiece Theater*. It was first-class drama that exposed the American public to great literature. Third, Mobil regularly bought space on the editorial page of the New York Times to make its case for why it and the industry had America's interest at heart and priced its products so that it could provide better products in the future. A senior public relations executive at Mobil, Herb Schmertz, wrote most of these "adatorials." Those three things, much like McKinsey's three-pronged effort to position itself as a leadership factory, made a difference to Mobil's standing and image.

What do I mean when I say Rawleigh wanted to humanize Mobil to its customers? Wasn't this just public relations? I don't think it was. Rawleigh gave some real thought to the idea that big international companies need to live up to their obligations to their customers and that customers need to understand Mobil's business. It was not what we now call corporate social responsibility. It was much more a justification of capitalism. And somehow the three things Mobil did added up. Maybe what they got right was the distance they wanted to travel on the humanity dimension. The adatorials never said profits were unimportant. The new gas stations were designed in the end for customers to pump more gas more comfortably. You don't have to move to the extreme end of a new dimension. You may not be believable if you do. Just know where you need to be and devise a program of integrated efforts to get there.

The last time I saw Rawleigh, he visited our house to attend an "installation" party for a 2-ton, 8-foot-high bronze sculpture Pamela and I commissioned for our living room. It was designed and built by Charles Perry, a well-known and highly regarded American sculptor.

When Pamela and I first saw the piece as a maquette, we asked Charlie what he was doing. He said, "I'm building equations in space." I had taken courses at Harvard on multi-dimensional function spaces so I really tuned in. Charlie's sculpture, two lines chasing one another, fills one entire cube in Johnson's rectilinear space perfectly with both power and elegance. I never get tired of looking at it and it looks different from every angle as you walk around it and the house. Maybe I am stretching the metaphor, but I suggest again that marketers are space benders. They see the possibilities of new dimensions as well as new dimensions within old ones.

The question for a marketer, or a CEO for that matter, is not only is there a new and powerful dimension lurking out there, but how soon do you need to pursue it? Often, it is sooner than you think. That was the essential message of Clay Christiansen's book *The Innovator's Dilemma*. The primary example in that book is the disk drive industry. Christiansen shows how the dimension that determined purchase decisions, density, changed to durability. Why? Because of the growing importance of mobile devices. At first, this mobile market looked small and unlikely to change buying factors. In a few years, it shifted everything. Very few, if any, of the manufacturers who made disks that sold on their density survived the transition. Christiansen points out that they paid too much attention to their big customers. There is a lesson here. If you are looking for a new dimension to the market-space, don't ask your big customers.

What makes the pace of these transitions hard to gauge is the underlying technologies. My McKinsey partner, Dick Foster, wrote *Innovation: The Attacker's Advantage*. In the book, Dick tracked the functionality of a new technology against the resources put into its development. Not against time, but money. The result was an S-curve. Progress is slow at first, then accelerates and then slows down as the new technology peters out. Making things more complicated, there is another S-curve that tracks how much a customer appreciates the new functionality. People slowly learn to love the new benefits, then can't get enough of them, but soon enough is enough. How much of those new optical brighteners can you really see in your laundry? The combined result of these two curves is that marketers' reaction time gets compressed. You may have only a few years before the eighth most important buying factor in an outlying segment becomes the first in the biggest segment of the market.

The toughest challenge to seeing new dimensions is you and your colleagues. You are what you sell. A BCG partner and friend of mine, Luc du Brabandere, wrote *The Forgotten Half of Change*. In the book, he argues that if you want to change, you must change twice. You must change reality as well as perception. Picture the couple, he says, that is always late. They may change reality by setting their clocks ahead, lightening their calendars, etc. But unless they change their perception of how rude it is to be late, says Luc, they will be late again.

I would have enjoyed being around Michelin when they decided to change the focus of their tires from handling and tread wear to safety—a totally different dimension and identity for the company. Having owned four Jaguars, I thought Michelin was wrong. Tires were manly, cool products for would-be race car drivers. I was wrong. The new dimension opened a much bigger market. But how did Michelin get their people to stop thinking Jaguar and Aston Martin, and start thinking Fords, families and safety? That's when the CEO becomes the chief marketer because the first job is to sell yourself on the new direction. What are you truly about? As a footnote, I noticed that recently Michelin has come back to the handling/tread wear dimension. Perhaps the sports car segment or pseudo sports car segment of the market is too attractive for them to ignore.

What, really, was the new dimension that Rawleigh Warner was trying to define and explore for Mobil? What does it mean to humanize a brand? Maybe the toughest challenge to defining and communicating a new dimension is getting the right level of abstraction. In the mid-'80s, Ohmae walked into my office, looked at me and said, "Convenience." This was like that scene in *The Graduate* when Benjamin's neighbor tells him plastics are the future. I said to Ken, "Convenience?" He said markets for consumer products will be dominated by convenience. Functionality, say 8 cups vs. 10, will be secondary selling attributes. Just touch the button and let it go. Just spray it on, just pour it down the drain. I thought it was interesting that Ohmae, trained as a nuclear physicist with an MBA from MIT, was so excited about what would sell toasters in the future. But he was. He saw what new technology could do and was going to do. Thus, he saw convenience as a big new theme and dimension of market-spaces. And he was right. But you have to be careful not to be too abstract. What does convenience really mean? How do you make it sufficiently concrete so your product designers understand what is convenient rather than just a novelty? We see this today with purported new dimensions such as sustainability and organic. What does organic mean? Or sustainable? Does BMW really expect to sell more cars because 16 percent of its batteries can be recycled? There are many false dimensions, mirrors rather than glass. But there are also many possibilities to be explored. The biggest mistake a young marketer can make is to assume that the space has been mapped, the matrix has been set and its dimensions permanently defined.

Johnny Cash didn't. Remember that scene in *Walk the Line*? Johnny had developed a serious pill habit and finally kicked it. He decides to redirect his singing career partly as a result of his struggles. He finds more direction when he reads his fan mail and sees that a lot of his fans are in prison. One morning, he walks into the office of the CEO of his record company dressed entirely in black and announces that he wants to record a live album in Folsom prison. Here's the script.

CEO: "While Johnny was out recuperating, the world changed.

Dylan's gone electric.

The Beatles are electric.

Hell, everybody's electric.

He needs a fresh sound and all he wants to do is cut a live album with the same old pickers at a maximum-security penitentiary."

Cash: "You can talk to me, you know. I'm standing right here."

CEO: "And what's with the black? It's depressing. It looks like you're going to a funeral."

Cash: "Maybe I am."

CEO: "Your fans are church folk, Johnny. They don't want to hear you singing to a bunch of murderers and rapists."

Cash: "Well, they're not Christians then."

CEO: "I'm fine with you doing a live album. Just not in prison."

Cash: "January 13th. I'll be in Folsom prison with June (Carter) and the boys. You listen to the tapes. You don't like them, you can toss them."

I suppose you could say that all Cash really did was extend the country music segment—which was aimed at losers, heartbreakers and the brokenhearted—to real screw-ups, thugs and felons. But to me, he did more. He revived his career based on some kind of epiphany he experienced when he gave up drugs. He found new conviction and courage based on personal experience. He was a marketer.

7

POETS &
LINGERIE

WHEN I SAW PAMELA for the first time, I had one thing on my mind. Why wouldn't I? She had the best legs I had ever seen. Legs that started at the bottom and ended at the top. Legs that belonged in seamed nylons or nothing at all. Legs that made you grind your teeth. I was finishing my workout with push-ups, as usual. Lying exhausted on the floor face-down, I looked up and saw these black high-top tennis shoes with pink shoelaces. By the time I worked my way up to the knees, I was in love. This is to say nothing about the rest of her. She is now 64 and still looks great—a result, I guess, of solid Czechoslovakian genes, a good diet and lots of exercise. She looks like a Victoria's Secret model with muscles.

She was and still is a divorce attorney. She has had her own practice for the last 20 years. Her last name is Valentine, which she kept after we got married. Valentine, divorce attorney.

I once suggested she add a slogan, something like "Let me help you drive a stake through her/his heart." And then added she could team up with a dating service to offer a full matchmaking and unmaking product line. She did not follow my advice. All her clients come from referrals. Her clientele is about 50/50 men and women. She is tough on them and makes sure they know the law and don't get greedy, which, near as I can tell, is the biggest problem in divorces. She keeps them out of court. We didn't get a prenup when we got married. But we just celebrated our 30th anniversary, so, so far so good.

Unlike Pamela, some divorce attorneys position themselves as assassins. And some clients want that, particularly when they are angry or feel betrayed. It often backfires as it does in other professional services such as lobbying. I have a friend who differentiates his firm, both growing and successful, by saying it "aggressively" serves its clients' interests. And only their interests. That may work, but it may not be smart. If you serve Uber, for example, or Google, do you fight for them or fight for several constituents and a long-term win-win resolution of different issues? More on this later.

Pamela, also known as Slim, is a very good cook. She assiduously collects and files recipes. One of our favorite dishes is rabbit. If you don't know it, try it. The meat is very clean and low fat. On a lark one year, Pamela decided to serve rabbit for Easter dinner. That wasn't enough. When our guests arrived, she greeted them dressed in a Playboy bunny outfit. High heels, fishnet stockings, little white cottontail, the whole works. Yes, I am a man who has been able to live his dreams.

Since I retired and she closed her office in New York a few years ago, we have fallen into the habit of splitting a six-pack of beer every morning—Elephant beer from Denmark. I've lost about 10 pounds. I have no idea why. Now, I'm not saying that a morning beer diet is for everyone, but maybe there is a sizeable segment of beer drinkers out there who like real beer and could be persuaded without much trouble that it's nutritious, even a health food. Is this a new dimension for the beer market? For alcohol in general?

You might be skeptical. Maybe most beer drinkers would be. But think about the evolution of the beer market. It used to be national and local. Bud and whatever local beer was available. Then there were a few regional beers. Rolling Rock, Coors. Light beer was the first significant new dimension and segment. The appeal was not quite about health. It was pitched as "less filling" more than fewer calories, but both were selling points. Currently, the new dimension of the beer market is called "craft," a follow-on to microbreweries. That means very local, not quite organic, small and special. An India Pale Ale from a place down the street.

Even though beer sales the last several years have been weak, IPA sales have taken off. All kinds of producers are popping up. They seem to limit their distribution and promotion. It's a word-of-mouth market. Pamela and I spent 30 minutes with the guy who stocks the newly expanded beer aisle of our local supermarket. He knew more about beer than most sommeliers know about wine. He noted that freshness is an important dimension for buyers, but the more expensive and darker craft beers now emphasize their vintage. He told us he gave his nephew a 2015 something or other. Alcohol is the big new dimension. The first question IPA drinkers ask is what percentage of alcohol is in the beer. Last summer, however, the current pitch was low-alcohol beer that is supposed to be more "thirst-quenching." The prices for these precious and exclusive brews are quite high. Some bottles cost $10 to $15 or more. Their names are imaginative and irreverent, sometimes politically incorrect. Even the distributors go by names like Remarkable Liquids. I think Slim and I are drinking more IPAs than Elephants these days. (Check out Resin; 9 percent alcohol by volume. Its slogan is "Beer is Culture.") For us, this change in our beer preferences is Kuhnian, the equivalent of a paradigm shift.

But why not sell beer as nutritious? Why can't health be a new dimension of the beer market-space? Could a beer maker sell that idea and legitimately claim to make a product that is healthier than other beers? I don't know. But why not explore it? What would a share point be worth? Do the math, do the research and maybe take a risk.

The question is, how do you find a genuinely new and powerful dimension and then own it? Anybody can play, incumbents as well as newcomers. Budweiser has done a good job of adding an emotional element to its beer. Those dogs and horses at Christmas time and during the Super Bowl. It's a God bless America beer. There are many opportunities to add an emotional dimension to a market-space.

After McKinsey, I joined BCG as the partner responsible for innovation, marketing and communications. I ran that unit with George Stalk. His book on "time-based competition" is a classic. One Friday in Boston, he said to me, "Instead of going home tonight, let's fly down to Nashville for the weekend where the consumer practice is meeting. It's run by a guy named Michael Silverstein. I want you to meet him." I called Pamela, asked for permission and headed off to Nashville with George. At the meeting, I heard for the first time about a concept called the "democratization of luxury." The idea was that there is a lot of room to increase the price of your product if you add an element of luxury to its benefits.

Over a drink, a good Barolo, Michael told me a story that captured the concept. He had a client whose major product was bug spray. You can probably guess. Michael asked the CEO to visit some customers with him. There was initial hesitation, but Michael persuaded him. So, they find themselves in a trailer park on a hot summer day.

"You sure we need to do this? I know my customers," says the CEO. "No, you don't," says Michael. They go inside the trailer home to visit with a woman in her 50s, a large woman sitting in her rocking chair with a fan whirring behind her. They thank her for her time and start talking about life in general and then get onto the subject of bug spray. As they are talking, guess what starts walking across the floor toward the woman? No kidding, the largest roach either of them has ever seen. Michael said they weren't sure what they should do. Should they interrupt the conversation and mention to the woman that a bug the size of a tank was making its way toward her? But she solved the problem for them. Without missing a beat, she got up from her chair, reached into a cabinet, took out a can of bug spray, their bug spray, went over to the roach, held the nozzle about 3 inches over it and started to spray. Michael said that both he and his client counted: one thousand one, one thousand two, one thousand three, one thousand four, one thousand five. Nozzle off. Michael said he doesn't think the roach died from the chemicals in the spray. "It drowned."

He went over to the woman, leaned down and asked, "What was that?"

She looked at him and said, "That was my first husband."

Michael swears this is true. And the client did, in fact, change its marketing message. Instead of highlighting the product's toxicity, his company began to highlight how the product—I hate to use the word—empowers you and protects you. You are the queen of your castle, not just a bug buster.

A few years after I met Michael, I worked with him on a book entitled *Trading Up*. In his book, he expanded on his idea that it was often possible to offer customers a new, more affordable level of luxury. The Limited, one of his clients, had sponsored his research on democratization. Michael argued that new luxury often had three different kinds of benefits: technical, functional and emotional. The trick was to get all three right. His primary example was one of the Limited's holdings, Victoria's Secret (VS). Michael explains how VS pursued all three. I won't go into the details here because it is all in the book, but the lingerie VS offered was, first, technically better than that of its competitors. There is apparently a lot of engineering in those panties and bras. As a result of the technology and their research into what young women want their lingerie to do for them, the functionality of VS products was dramatically improved. (I'm treading carefully here.) Finally, VS hired some very good-looking and slender models to appear in their catalogues. The sex appeal went through the roof.

VS could offer superior lingerie at a price point well below luxury brands such as La Perla. Its promotion and advertising basically said you can wear sexy lingerie seven days a week, not just on weekends, and not break the bank. The technical, functional and emotional changes were all definitive improvements and they added up to a new dimension—call it everyday sexiness and self-esteem. As with the bug spray, emotion played a big role in redefining the product. But the technical and functional dimensions were important factors as well. The lesson for marketers may be to explore all three options as you think about levers to deliver a new dimension to your customers.

Given the prices VS charges for its products, young women can afford to buy more lingerie. So can older women. There was a time when there were few days at our house when a catalogue or a package from VS didn't arrive. I'm not complaining.

The Limited did not discover the luxury dimension of the lingerie market. But it found a new point on the spectrum that ran from everyday to only-on-special-occasions and then delivered value (benefits minus costs) at a price that young women were willing to pay. On the other hand, when "instant" photography became available, it represented a genuinely new dimension for an established market. I was struck by a story I read in Harvard Magazine recently ("The Polaroid Moment," March-April 2017) about Edwin Land.

Here's an excerpt: "Land's daughter, on a family vacation in Santa Fe in 1943, asked, in his words, 'why she could not see at once the picture I had taken of her...Within the hour, the camera, the film, and the physical chemistry became so clear to me' that he discussed it all with the company's patent attorney." The technology was basically available. But the insight about the dimension of time had not been.

Did Land understand that he was inaugurating our brave new world of selfies? Probably not. But he certainly saw the technical, functional and emotional aspects of what he was doing. From the same article: "He was clear that the 'aesthetic purpose' of his photographic system is to make available a new medium of expression...to individuals who have an artistic interest in the world around them."

Pamela and I recently bought a wonderful photograph done in the style of a classic Vogue fashion shot. It represents the past space of photography when the quality of the image was all that mattered. Were we fools? No. We just represent the old segment that still exists and is probably still vibrant. But for "photography" today, time matters. And the new dimension resulted from relaxing a constraint that incumbent players accepted as a given. Maybe you can tell a similar story about sound. Quality and format dominated the music space. But the Walkman brought the dimension of place. The sound moved with you. You were not confined to your living room. Was this what Ohmae was talking about when he told me that convenience would be an uber-dimension? My guess is that if we recreated our conversation today, he would say "intelligence" rather than convenience. As software becomes a key aspect of the functionality of products and services, consumers will expect it to think and serve them in new ways. That's what seems to be happening with cars. Cars park themselves now and they keep drivers from drifting into adjacent lanes. Pretty soon, experts say, cars will drive themselves. I'm skeptical, but wed that functionality to new business models like Uber, and the whole automotive space is likely to change dramatically. It will become much less personal as "ownership" disappears. Why own a car when you can just call one? Will you care how long it takes to get to 60 MPH or how well it handles? What does all this mean for Michelin and its tires? For the new marketer, I wonder if "intelligence" is the right dimension or some lower level of abstraction?

New dimensions don't always bring unblemished value. Sometimes there are benefits lost along established dimensions. Pamela and I were flying to our place in West Palm not long ago when I ran out of something to read. She gave me one of her cooking magazines, Saveur, and I started reading a chicken recipe. I'm a simple person. Then I noticed an article next to the recipe about what happened to the chicken market in the U.S. after WWII. During the war, people ate lots of chicken because beef and pork were in short supply. Chicken producers were worried that after the war people would stop eating chicken, which was kind of a skinny, unappetizing bird back then. So, says the article, with the backing of A&P, the USDA and poultry organizations, a guy named Howard Pierce started a public relations campaign, the heart of which was a contest dubbed, "The Chicken of Tomorrow" and a film entitled *Chicken Every Sunday* starring a child actress named Natalie Wood. You can't make this stuff up. The winning birds were "so top-heavy that they walk like a fat man trying to kick a field goal in a telephone booth."

A billion-dollar market was born because fat breasts became the essential dimension of a chicken. Okay, maybe it was just a product attribute and not a big new dimension, but it was a pretty dramatic change in the product. The article reads, "There is no question that his effort was a technological and scientific success that spawned an entire industry, cut prices, and dramatically altered our day to day eating habits." The only trouble was the new chickens tasted lousy and had to be dressed up with all kinds of spices. And the birds were "grown" under pretty disgusting conditions. The article concludes that now the race is on for a different kind of chicken, one that is treated humanely and tastes good. Like a skinny Bresse chicken in France. What you learn on airplanes! I was surprised the article did not mention Frank Perdue, who found ways to significantly improve the quality of his chickens and charge a premium. Like VS, he innovated throughout the value chain: everything from egg hatching and chicken feeding to refrigerated trucks so his chicken was never frozen. Finding a new dimension that creates value in the middle of a market may be the way to go.

There are plenty of examples. Until a few years ago, Canon, the camera maker, essentially had two segments: point-and-shoot cameras that cost less than $100 and the professional cameras with plenty of complexity that cost over $300. Like VS, Canon found a middle segment, one they thought could be quite large, that offered sharp 35MM quality in a simple-to-use camera at a price between $150 and $200. Canon believed it could deliver those cameras and it did with the AE1. It changed what photography was about.

In my second year at HBS in a course on advertising, the professor assigned a case on "net unduplicated reach." He asked the student next to me, a friend, to begin the case—to lay out both the argument and the issues. If you get called on, it helps if you have read the case. My friend had not. He loved opera and my guess is he had spent the evening before listening to Maria Callas rather than doing his homework. He declined the professor's invitation. Even though I had read the case, I didn't want to show up my friend so I looked steadily downward. It didn't work. "Mr. Matassoni, would you like to begin?"

"Yes sir. This case is unusual because it is about a concept rather than a company or a specific problem. The concept is called net unduplicated reach. The basic argument is that if you are responsible for buying media for a product or service, you can maximize the effect of your budget on sales by reaching as many people as possible, even if you reach them only once."

"Thank you. Did you find yourself agreeing with this approach?"

"I found it to be a compelling but limited idea."

I was hoping he would turn his attention to another student, but he decided to stick with me.

"Would you care to share with us why?"

"I wondered if some products or services required more than one exposure to an ad to move a potential customer from consideration to purchase. Maybe this is a good idea for impulse purchases rather than products for which the buying decision is complicated or takes time."

"Anything else?"

"I wondered what the media buyer should do post launch. What does he do down the road when most of the potential buyers have been reached? Does he ignore them and persist in reaching those last few living in far-away valleys, or does he change his tactics and reinforce heavy users?"

"What else?"

"Well, you may not find this a rational argument, but I thought advertising was more than math."

His expression changed. This was no longer a drill for him. Had I possibly said something that interested him? Even some of my classmates seemed to awaken.

"Don't you think advertising should be a quantitative, disciplined function?"

"Of course. But I would like to believe that advertising is both an art and a science. Something to which someone's heart as well as head needs to be brought to bear. Something that combines both logic and emotion. Something that moves our souls as well as appeals to our reason."

"Whoa! Whence comes this plea for art and emotion? Do you want us to return to the glory days of Madison Avenue when the creatives ruled the world and nothing mattered except the perfect plea and memorable tagline?"

"Nope, all I am saying is that the modern advertising man or, for that matter, the modern marketer needs to integrate his sensibilities to excel. He needs to defeat the dilemma Eliot described in his essay on the metaphysical poet Cowley."

I was in danger of losing him.

"Pray tell us more, Mr. Matassoni, about Eliot and this essay."

"Eliot admired the metaphysical poets–Donne, Herbert, Cowley– because they used elaborate metaphors, conceits, to convey complex messages and emotion. He cited Herbert, for example, who compared a dangerous sea journey to a compass and his wife to the fixed foot of that compass, which would bring him home safely. Eliot also believed that modern poets and man in general suffered from a 'dissociation of sensibilities.' Man, he said, could no longer think and feel at the same time."

The accountants in the room were dazed.

"Well, I can assure you that in my 20 years of teaching this course, that's the first time someone has mentioned metaphysical poetry. So, what do we conclude before we open this discussion up to your classmates?"

"We conclude that the modern manager sometimes should make business a mission, not a solution. He should put down his calculator and listen to opera."

My friend next to me gave me a thumbs-up. He knew exactly what I meant. Reach for the stars, not for the numbers. Even if the stars are just bug spray or deodorant.

When I was at BCG, I worked with a partner, Philip Evans, who argued that as the cost of bandwidth plummeted, the trade-off between richness (the quality and complexity of the interactions with customers) and reach would become much less of a compromise because of the emergence of what he and others called Internet 2.0. John Hagel, another of my former colleagues and friends at McKinsey, defined 2.0 as "an emerging network centric platform to support distributed, collaborative and cumulative creation by its users." Evans also argued that one key aspect of richness was the feedback one can now get from customers and potential customers, so much feedback that the distinction between producer and consumer had become obsolete. You can know, for example, how much of a new product to make before you sell it. He cited a company called Threadless.

"There is a website called Threadless.com for T-shirt enthusiasts. You join Threadless by registering and giving your T-shirt size. You can look at, literally, thousands of T-shirts designed by members of the Threadless community. You can develop ideas based on other people's designs. You can import designs via cut-and-paste techniques from other sources, and you can post your T-shirt for everybody to praise or criticize. Threadless holds 'beauty contests' for T-shirts rather than their models. Members of the Threadless community critique each other's work, rate the submission 1-5 and indicate whether if manufactured, they would buy it. At the end of each 10-day period, Threadless closes the contest, announces the winners and then manufactures the winning shirts in numbers proportional to the expressed buying intentions. They sell those T-shirts, which cost $13 to manufacture, for $20. Sixty-thousand T-shirts a month. That's $14 million annualized, $5 million gross profits. They have 20 employees, $250,000 revenue per professional. Not bad."

This is a long way from Victoria's Secret's high-tech, sexy lingerie with its beautiful models, runways and catalogues. But it may be that VS's future competitor might use some kind of Threadless model—business model, that is. And maybe us guys will be involved in the voting!

We could also vote for beer. How about a Starbucks-like chain where customers gather to read Sports Illustrated and Road and Track? Where there are hundreds of IPAs and ales from all over the world on tap. Where there are contests every hour or so for the best-tasting beers. Where "hoppy" and "citrus" are common denominators. And every day or week, there would be a thought on a big chalkboard about the importance of beer. Something like this:

"A herd of buffalo can move only as fast as the slowest buffalo. When the herd is hunted, it is the slowest and weakest ones at the back that are killed first. This natural selection is good for the herd as a whole because the general speed and health of the whole group keeps improving by the regular culling of the weakest members. In much the same way, the human brain can operate only as fast as the slowest brain cell. Excessive intake of alcohol, we all know, kills brain cells, but naturally it attacks the slowest and weakest brain cells first. In this way, regular consumption of beer eliminates the weakest brain cells, making the brain a faster and more efficient machine. That's why you always feel smarter after a few beers."

There could be contests for the best chalkboard contributions. What was the best thing Ernest Hemingway said about beer? What would Ayn Rand have said about beer?

To go back to my premise: emotional involvement in the product or service is prime territory for competition and growth. The discovery and delivery of new market dimensions may in the future be a much more collaborative effort and the nature of the collaborations will itself be a potential new dimension—as much so as the actual product or service. Reputation, authenticity and trust will be factors in these new "communities" we used to call market segments. Brave new world.

8

THE FINAL YEARS
AT MCKINSEY

*M*OST MARKETING DIRECTORS keep their jobs for two to three years. I stayed at McKinsey for almost 20, 18 as a partner. My initial portfolio included public, press and alumni relations. Around 1985, I was asked to take over the McKinsey Quarterly, which was a pretty modest publication that carried no original material. I hired one of the best young editors from the Harvard Business Review, Alan Kantrow, to come in and make it into something and he did. Within a few years, the Quarterly was filled with original articles as well as research. Alan was elected a partner for his work. He wasn't just smart (summa at Harvard); he had character and courage and raised the bar for us. I was given a lot of credit for bringing him into the firm.

When I first talked to Ron Daniel about joining McKinsey, I said that the job was probably going to be more internal communications than external marketing. I was wrong at first. But gradually that came to be. I'm pretty sure that the biggest contribution I made to McKinsey was the improvements I helped to make to our internal communications.

About the time I took over the Quarterly, Fred Gluck asked me to develop a knowledge management system. There was nothing in place. If a consultant wanted to know what we knew collectively about some management issue, he called around to people in relevant practices and hoped their secretaries could help him find documents, articles, etc. that were somewhere in a file drawer. Even basic information about clients was on file cards in a room in New York. Fred's only advice was to make sure to guard confidential information and design the system so our consultants talked to each other rather than just reading papers and trying to apply the ideas on their own. And that's what I did, with tremendous help from a young guy named Brook Manville whom I met through an alumnus. Brook went to Yale and then Oxford. What convinced me to hire him was he did his thesis at Oxford on the role of city states in ancient Greece. I concluded he would understand McKinsey because, in many ways, it was a global collection of city states. Brook, too, was eventually elected a partner for his work and toughness. He had many partners tell him he was wasting McKinsey's resources because they had personal access to all the people and thinking they needed to know. They were wrong, of course. Fred backed Brook and me.

Basically, we put two systems in place. One contained information on clients and the nature of our engagements. The other was a source of documents that practices designated as shareable and useful. There were about 2,000 of them that we stored in depots in New York, London and Sydney. That way, we could overnight them to teams, who always wanted them the next day. We named the whole thing PDNet. We tracked what was ordered—what was "selling." Marketing wasn't. Pricing was.

By 1996, there were 12,000 documents on PDNet. Every month, at least 2,000 of them were sent to teams. Making the best sellers' list was considered an important contribution to McKinsey. The new systems changed people's behavior. They also changed how we thought of ourselves—our identity. We were more than great consultants, gunslingers who could solve any problem. We were part of a broad body of knowledge and experience, and it was our obligation to bring it to bear on every assignment. Brook helped McKinsey change twice: in reality and in self-perception. Our work was written up as a Harvard Business School case.

That wasn't enough for Fred. One Friday morning, he called me into his office and handed me some papers.

"What do you think?"

I gave them a quick read. They were memos about recent practice meetings.

"I don't like them."

"Why?"

"Because all they're saying is we are spending money on practice meetings in nice places. Not all our partners think that's a good investment."

"Okay, Mr. Smarty Pants. Why don't you fix them?"

I called Bill Price, my longtime editor and right-hand man, and told him we would be doing some work over the weekend. First, we figured out the format. One page, not white, printed front and back. Title (not cute, short), five paragraphs with sidebars. First paragraph, here's a problem you will likely encounter (like organization design, logistics, etc.). Second, here is how we typically think about that problem. Third, here's a different way. Fourth, here are the titles of a couple of documents you can read if you're interested. They are on PDNet. Fifth, here are the names of people you can call.

Monday morning, as expected, Fred called. I went to his office and handed him five practice "bulletins." He read them, not looking up.

He said, "These are not good." Then, looking up with a big smile, he added, "These are great!"

So we launched the bulletins, and sent out one or two a week. A woman named Ellen Nenner managed the process and really delivered. She also put the last brick in place: the KRD. Our consultants needed a quick reference guide to all the practices, which then numbered over 20. Ellen started to produce a little red book we named the Knowledge Resource Directory. Names, phone numbers, documents, you name it. It was an instant hit. Ellen carefully revised it every six months. Remember that ad that ended with the slogan, "Don't leave home without it?" The KRD was in every consultant's briefcase.

What was really going on was that Fred was moving McKinsey toward a dual mission. He finally said it out loud in a memo to all partners in 1993.

"There are two ways to look at McKinsey. The most common way is that we are a client service firm whose primary purpose is to serve companies seeking our help. That's legitimate. But I believe there is an even more powerful way for us to see ourselves. We should begin to view our primary purpose as building a great institution that becomes an engine for producing highly motivated world-class people who will in turn serve our clients extraordinarily well."

The knowledge management systems we built were not about knowledge. They were about people.

Some time in the early '90s, Fred wrote a memo that came to be called the "airplane memo." He describes one of our young partners sitting down next to a CEO on a plane. After a while, they start talking and the CEO says to him, "What are you and McKinsey thinking about these days?" And the partner basically says, "Oh, you know, competitive advantage and stock valuation." The CEO presses and says, "Okay, but what's on your mind? What are you exploring?" And the partner doesn't have much to say. Fred basically says you shouldn't be a partner unless you can have a substantive conversation about something you really care about. He says you can't be a good generalist unless you are a specialist in something important. He adds, unless you can talk for several hours with the CMO, CSO or CFO about his job, keep your mouth shut until you can. The goal, he says, is not that you can talk for several hours, but that you can listen for that long, guide the conversation, and humbly make suggestions. So, you can be wise and helpful, not just smart. So you can really own the problem, not the "solution." It reminded me of the yellow pad notes that one of our senior partners used to write to his client.

Marvin always stressed that McKinsey was "one firm" around the world. Ron reinforced that during his 12 years as managing partner. And of course Fred did with his focus on building and sharing our knowledge. He never stopped trying to enhance our sense of self as a powerful and bonded team. He loved the idea. One morning he reminded me that our annual partner conference was coming up and asked if I could figure out how to celebrate our 50th anniversary. I thought about it and decided we could leverage the oral history Ron had started and I had continued. I spent hour after hour listening to the tapes of our past and current senior partners. Fortunately I had had them indexed so I could search for themes like how and why did we decide to go international. Finally, with Fred's urging, we got the "show" down to 12 minutes. Just voices, loud and clear. The first voice was Marvin's. "I was born in Cleveland, Ohio in 1896. And then voice after voice told the audience where the speaker was born. And then they said a little more and more and more of McKinsey's story was told.

"I was born in Munich. It was after the war. I had tuberculosis."–this from the powerful head of our German office.

"We opened our office in Mayfair and sat around. The phone didn't ring."

"We were told by the potential client that we would report to the COO. Marvin turned it down."

I added slides of early partners from the '40s and '50s and going forward. Pictures of them on the golf course in their three-piece suits. Pictures of them with their wives at McKinsey gatherings.

But something was missing. I asked Gene Zelazny, a brilliant communications specialist in our New York office, to take a look. He suggested I add music. I said, Gene, you have to be kidding. We have never had music in a McKinsey presentation. We tried it. Dionne Warwick, "That's What Friends Are For." Pamela came with me to the partners' conference. There we were in the control booth with our two slide projectors, a dissolve unit and a tape recorder. The lights went down and from the first moment you could hear a pin drop. The music became an interlude between past and future. After it ended, the partners heard more voices, now from new parts of our growing empire. "I was born in Argentina. I was born in Hong Kong." Then a voice asked,

"What will we do when Marvin is gone?"

At the end of the show, people stood up, applauded and began to embrace each other. There were tears. It was probably one of the happiest moments of my career at McKinsey. That little low-tech slide show solidified the partners' sense of who we were, where we came from and where we were headed.

Externally, through the '80s and mid-'90s, we managed to keep McKinsey outside the boxing ring of consultants even though we would occasionally be brought back to earth. In late '84, for example, my friend Steve Prokesh called to say he had written a cover story for Business Week on the track record of the companies we had extolled in *In Search of Excellence*. The track record was not very good. His article was fair and correctly assessed the weaknesses in our research, but it didn't do any damage to McKinsey's standing. Maybe everyone already knew that success doesn't last. And maybe when you are outside the ring, it doesn't matter.

One night, after the stock market crashed in 1987, I got home to find a message from an editor at the Journal whom I had dated, which said, "Honey, your man Ohmae made a fool of himself on TV tonight." It turned out Ohmae had appeared on Ted Koppel's Nightline. The show was an hour, 45 minutes of which were devoted to American experts like Nobel winner Robert Solow, who tried to explain why the market crashed. Then there was 10 minutes with the head of the Bundesbank. Then a concluding five minutes with Ohmae. Koppel asked him the same question: "Why the big drop?" Ohmae says because the real markets of the world are significantly overshadowed by financial markets and trading. Koppel asks, "How much bigger are these financial flows than the flows of real goods and services?" Ohmae says it's like trying to stuff "D-size dollars in an A-size cup." Koppel is, to say the least, nonplussed. Solow comes to his rescue and asks, "Mr. Ohmae, do you have any more lingerie examples to explain the world economy?"

The next week, Business Week reported on the show and said Ohmae was the only guy who had much to say. Again, it helps to be outside the ring—to be a unique institution with unique people.

In Germany, we continued to get bad press because of all the cost-cutting work we did there. The unions hated us. But by the late '80s, the work of the McKinsey Global Institute allowed us to shift the discussion to productivity. Our basic counter-message became that countries need to be competitive in a global economy. As they say in Mad Men, "If you don't like what they are saying about you, change the conversation."

One morning about that time, I got a call from a couple of our partners in Italy. They said they wanted some advice. I asked if we could talk over the phone. They said no. So the following week, I flew to Milan. Our office arranged for me to spend the night in a new Ritz Carlton, which had been built on the site of an ancient nunnery. My suite must have once been a chapel. It was huge and seemed almost sacred. Maybe I should have prayed for wisdom given what the next day brought.

I sat down with three of my Italian partners in the morning. They said they had two related questions. One, should they bribe the press? Two, should they give them information about our clients that reporters frequently asked for? Apparently, some of our competitors did both. McKinsey was the largest strategy consultant in Italy and very strong in the financial sector. It possessed information that various "investors" would find quite valuable.

I think my partners knew what the answers to their questions would be. No. We were not going to follow prevailing country practice. We would set our own rules and deal from a position of strength. But they wanted me to corroborate their gut instincts. I, on the other hand, didn't want to lecture them about professional values or remind them of our policies in the U.S. Even though we believed all our offices belonged to "one firm," that didn't mean we were all the same. So we sat around for most of the morning circling the questions. First, we asked, "What would Marvin do?" Then we asked, "What does professional mean? What is in the best interests of our clients? Of McKinsey? Short term, long term?" They did not ask me to cover for them should McKinsey get bad press by refusing to provide information. This was a private conversation among partners. Morning over. But the day was just beginning.

Another of our senior partners in Milan asked me to join him for lunch. We went to his club nearby. We sat in this beautiful, long, open-air dining room looking down on the Piazza del Duomo. The menu and food were wonderful; so was the wine.

I asked Roberto (not his real name), "How have you been?"

Roberto was a highly regarded member of our banking practice whom everyone liked.

"Good," he said. "I have been writing a book—an exposé of Berlusconi. That's what I wanted to talk to you about. It's finished and I am ready to publish it."

"Roberto, why? You put yourself at considerable personal risk."

"The man is despicable. I want my countrymen to know what I know about him."

"Do you really know things about him the country does not?"

"Yes."

"Look, I'll read the book on the flight home, but this is not the right territory for us. Yes, McKinsey now writes about policy and trade and regulation, but an attack on an active politician is too much. Even if you published your book anonymously, you would be found out."

I didn't like giving that advice because Roberto's intentions were good. He wasn't ego-driven. He cared about his country. I read his book on the way home; it was solid and revealing. But it was never published.

I continued to work with practice leaders the way I did when I joined McKinsey. You could do real work with them and make something happen, particularly the ones who understood we wanted to appear as leaders, not experts. Some became great friends and kept me committed to McKinsey even though I was beginning to suspect it was time for a change.

In the early '90s, I took on the task of putting some sort of competitive analysis in place. We were particularly interested in how we were doing in head-to-head competition. We had new engagement reports and people were happy to talk about wins. But we gathered no information on losses. Who would want to report that? Two young, really sharp women in our Boston office who wanted to work part-time to start families helped me to organize that effort. Again, we had to put new systems in place to get the information we wanted, and again Fred backed us. There were some surprises. Much to our chagrin, we found out that in some situations we were losing more engagements than we were winning. For example, we were getting killed by Bain on the West Coast. We debriefed the partners involved and found out why and made that information available. Before long, our win rates went up and we had real momentum in terms of our consultants' willingness to provide information about their defeats as well as their victories.

I brought in two more young editors to work on the Quarterly. One became editor-in-chief when Alan went off to Asia, basically to be me there. Then, of course, around 1990 it was time for McKinsey to develop a website. Our recruiting function developed our first site. Then I got the assignment to do more with it. We developed a global site, to which our country sites could link, and a site for the Quarterly. The global site was just a bunch of press clips, old and new. The Quarterly site contained everything that was in the Quarterly. We decided to give a lot of our knowledge and experience away on the Quarterly site rather than tantalize its visitors. That paid off for us in the long run. We learned that sometimes if you want to own an idea, you should give it away. Through the Quarterly and our press relations, we learned that clever research can be the best way to convey an idea. For example, our utilities practice produced a long, boring article on how to de-market energy. We didn't want to expose Quarterly readers to that kind of content. In general, we didn't want to publish industry-specific pieces, which tended to be best practice and not strategic or top management focused. So I asked John Sawhill if the practice could do some quick research on the backgrounds of CMOs at the biggest utilities. It turned out they were all environmentalists. Their approach to their job was basically to get customers to stop using energy–not get unprofitable customers to cut back their usage. We published the results rather than the article–200 words rather than 2,000. The business and industry press wrote a dozen articles about its implications. McKinsey owned the issue. We did the same thing in banking, electronics and other practices where we had strong relationships with practice leaders.

Not all went well. The two young editors started to become rivals after I nominated one for partner and he was elected. I failed to nip their quarrels in the bud and it hurt me later. McKinsey was very forgiving but not on people matters. One of my biggest screw-ups was totally my fault. I hired a PR firm to help our banking practice in New York. They got an article published in American Banker under the name of the head of the NY banking practice. They didn't understand that McKinsey, a true meritocracy, would never do something like that. If you wrote it, your name went on it. Worse, the article was already slated to be published in the Harvard Business Review under the real authors' names. HBR pulled the article when they heard about the American Banker piece.

None of this should have happened. I did what I could to make up for it. I reduced the article to 700 words. Roland Mann, our venerable and wise editor in London whom I had replaced as head of the Quarterly, generously rewrote the intro to focus on policy implications (it was about strategy under deregulation). The two authors quickly approved it and thanked me. I sent it to the Wall Street Journal to David Asman, whom I knew well and could ask for a quick assessment. The article appeared a few days later. Would you rather have an article in HBR or an editorial in the WSJ? Did I feel better? Yes. Did I still feel lousy and stupid? Yes. Did it kill me to be the recipient of such understanding and helpfulness from my colleagues? Yes. Did it make me cry because one of the authors had cancer and we lost him soon afterwards? What do you think?

I think I was getting bored and arrogant. I can't remember when but sometime in the mid-'90s I got a call from London from David Frost's people. They wanted to know if McKinsey would consider doing a television series that would involve David interviewing CEOs with a senior McKinsey partner providing background. I said we would even though I had for years opposed any sort of co-branding with another institution. So I had drinks with David at the Carlisle a couple of times when he was in New York and dinner with him and his wife at his restaurant in Mayfair. It was all swell and I enjoyed the conversations and I wanted to make it work. Maybe I was starstruck. I called Ian Davis, then the head of McKinsey's office in the U.K. and dropped by to see him. In a nice but firm way he said, "Bill, this is a mistake. This isn't McKinsey. In the end it might be entertaining, but it would be indiscreet. I am surprised you are even considering it." I was disappointed. But Ian was right. It would have been wrong to oppose him and push the project any further. Ian was highly regarded throughout McKinsey for good reasons and several years later he was elected managing partner.

So, looking back on all this, I've concluded that I was making a big mistake. I was managing but not leading. If I were leading, I would have more forcefully taken a position that McKinsey needed to dramatically cut down on its publishing. That our job was to produce not authors but authority. Yes, I presented data to the executive committee about how many business books were now being published each year and how shallow most of them were, but its response was that we should keep publishing. They didn't want to hear it. I should have realized I was no longer in touch with the partners running the firm.

Besides Marvin Bower, who was always my source of guidance on McKinsey values, I served two managing partners for whom I had a great deal of respect. Ron Daniel was the first. Ron was tall and looked every inch the managing partner. Elegant, well-spoken, intelligent, he pretty much let me find my way and intervened only on occasion to keep me out of trouble. The other managing partner was Fred Gluck, who took over in the late '80s after Ron. Fred was short and tough with a great big heart. I fought with him all the time, but he gave me the important assignments that shaped my career at McKinsey. Fred and I had a lot of fun together. I'd love to tell you some stories, like the time we landed in Kennedy at about six on a Saturday night and ended up at a party at Halston's place in Olympic Tower. We rode up with Gregory Peck and his wife. Fred and I were the only people who weren't famous. By 10, he was dancing with a blond bombshell who had just written a tell-all book. By 11, he was having a heated discussion with Liza Minnelli (what the hell were they arguing about?), and by 2 a.m., he was depositing the actress Karen Black into a cab. But enough. What happens in New York stays in New York.

Marvin gave McKinsey its values, Ron gave it its class and Fred gave it its love for ideas. But the next managing partner, Rajat Gupta, well, he gave it politics and greed. I am totally biased about this assessment because Rajat pushed me out of McKinsey.

McKinsey elects its managing partners every three years. They don't openly run for the job. It happens rather mysteriously, a little like electing the pope. The Europeans wanted a non-American. Gupta was Indian but had spent plenty of time in the U.S. So, we elected him. I didn't buy his act. He talked, for example, about the importance of growing the firm's knowledge, but when I checked our knowledge database, the one Brook and I had put in place, to see how many articles and ideas he had contributed, the number that popped up was zero. Nothing. When he spoke, it reminded me of Chauncey Gardiner (played by Peter Sellers) in the movie *Being There*. "In the spring, the garden will grow." We didn't agree on several issues. I thought we had begun to publish too much and that the quality was not consistent. He didn't want to say no to anyone. I thought we were violating our policies in a couple of important ways. In Germany, for example, we were letting our clients talk about our work in the press. We stopped asking them to keep our work confidential. Rajat wouldn't do anything about that. At Enron, we were spending considerable time in the boardroom, again something our policies forbade. When I told Rajat we needed to either change the policies or, better, our behavior, he wouldn't do anything. Where I had authority, I used it. The Enron team insisted we should publish an article in the Quarterly about their client and how uniquely good it was. Our policy was not to publish articles about specific companies. They wanted to ignore that policy. We didn't and their article never got written.

That said, the managing partner has a right to assemble his own team, and Rajat didn't want me on his team. And maybe I had become autocratic and stale after 20 years. I was told by the personnel committee that evaluated my performance that it was time for me to go. That I had stopped growing and needed a new career. "Take a year or so, but please leave."

And it was over, just like that. The year went by quickly. I remember taking the train home to New Canaan my last day, scared to death. How good was I? Good within McKinsey but not outside? Did I have any real skills? The alumni network I had helped to build was good at placing ex-consultants but not ex "administrative" consultants. BCG called me (word got around) and asked if I had any interest in joining them as a partner. I said yes. We had some good discussions. But when their managing partner, Carl Stern, called Rajat out of professional courtesy to let him know they were interested in me, Rajat asked Carl not to proceed because it would embarrass him. The guy was a prince.

But he was elected managing partner three times because the economy was good and partners were making lots of money. I was long gone when the headlines revealed that Gupta had been convicted of insider trading. He went to jail. He filed appeals, but they were denied. Ironically, McKinsey has recently taken his name off its official alumni list. Dishonest? I'd say so. McKinsey doesn't want to admit that even a leadership factory can produce a crook. I'm glad that Marvin passed away before he could see McKinsey's name dragged through the mud. And I'm glad, and lucky, that I got pushed out before all this happened.

So I lasted for almost twenty years at McKinsey, in part because I was pretty good at what I did and took on lots of new assignments, and in part because I had some great colleagues who gave me solid guidance and support.

9

ADVENTURES
IN E-COMMERCE
LA-LA LAND

*A*BOUT TWO MONTHS after leaving McKinsey, I found myself on the beach in Anguilla. Pamela and I always celebrated her birthday there. A bottle of champagne appeared at our door. Then I got a phone call from John Hogan. To say John was a crazy-smart Irishman doesn't begin to describe him. He was trustworthy and a great friend over the years. He asked me to consider cutting short the vacation and joining Mitchell Madison Group, a small consulting firm he and several other former McKinsey colleagues had founded.

"Why?"

"I can't tell you. Let's just say some investment bankers will be in the room."

I really didn't understand. The guys who started MMG were renegades. They represented the only major defection McKinsey had experienced. They had all been part of the banking practice. The heart of their strategy was to be number two next to McKinsey in serving financial institutions in the New York City arena. They focused on sourcing work. Believe it or not, banks buy a lot of paper despite all their investments in information technology. The strategy worked. Mitchell Madison grew to $200 million in revenues in four years. For every client, MMG analyzed the structure of its major suppliers. It used cost curves and other frameworks to develop a unique understanding of the suppliers' pricing and profits. It then used that knowledge to save its clients millions. They were a good example of a player in the upper right box of the process/impact matrix.

So, was there something wrong? One little thing. For every category of spending, MMG anointed one associate to be the world's most knowledgeable expert. He or she would help the consulting teams do their work quickly and powerfully. But soon MMG's rivals, the big accounting firms, for example, started to cherry pick these wunderkinds, offering them twice what they were making. MMG's knowledge base began to walk out the door. Growth started to slow. And the three lead partners started to squabble. They concluded it was time to sell the firm.

That's where I came in. I was going to help develop the "narrative" and write what is called the "green book" that investment bankers use to attract interest. Had I done anything like this before? Nope. The reason MMG called me was very simple. His name was Tom Steiner and he had founded MMG. I worked with Tom extensively at McKinsey. Among other things, I helped him write a book called *Technology in Banking: Creating Value and Destroying Profits.* The title basically captured the dilemma faced by financial institutions. They were spending huge amounts on IT but not gaining competitive advantage or widening their profit margins. Lots of client work resulted. Tom was intensely analytic and his book was filled with data. It just needed a story. He gave me a lot of credit for helping him and his colleagues.

So, a few months after leaving McKinsey and a few days from the beach in Anguilla, I found myself sitting in front of the entire consulting staff of MMG and a team of bankers. Tom announced that the partners had decided to sell the firm. He said they had all agreed to bring me in to help with the effort. Then he turned to me.

"Bill, would you like to give us your thoughts on this?"

I was not well prepared—tan, but not prepared. I said something about the fact that most management consulting firms sell for about one times revenues because future earnings were highly uncertain unless the firm had a record of strong relationships. Then I said I would be wandering the hallways talking to all of them and asked them to give some thought to how we could present MMG as more than a consulting firm and how we could enhance the value of our knowledge and skills. Sound familiar? We needed to get out of the consulting space if we wanted a multiple that was more than one. And we had some evidence that we were worth more. In one case, we aggressively negotiated a huge contract for semiconductor chips by leveraging MMG's knowledge of cost curves and when major new chunks of capacity were slated to come on line. We were players, not just analysts.

My first meeting with our investment bankers was disappointing. Their initial list of potential buyers had only consultants. The problem with that is if consulting firms sell for one times revenues, they were unlikely to pay more than that to buy another consulting firm. Eventually, we met with a broader list of suitors that included advertising and public relations conglomerates who were jealous of MMG's fees and its ability to serve competitors. We also met with high-tech manufacturers who wanted to be smarter about executing their pricing strategies. I pushed for meetings with software companies who might be able to combine their capabilities with MMG's. Some kind of brilliant combination of technology and brains. The bankers were not able to pitch that angle. I'm not sure there was one.

Meanwhile, I kept writing and rewriting the green book, trying to balance fantasy and reality. Every evening around six, one of the lead partners would visit and give me his latest thinking on our positioning. He would be followed by another partner and then another. There were several evenings when I ended up sleeping at my club because

I had missed the last train to New Canaan. But it paid off. Our joint thinking produced a compelling story. Then, a few months later, one cool Saturday morning in New York, we sold the firm. For 2.5 times its revenues. The buyer was USWeb/CKS, a roll-up of small IT firms and consultants, and a roll-up of communications and website experts. These firms were located all over the U.S. Headquarters was, where else, in Silicon Valley. MMG was going to add strategy to the mix. One-stop shopping for advice and implementation for the busy CEO. It wasn't very plausible and the deal was for stock, but everyone seemed to be happy. The stock was going up. We jumped on a plane in our suits and went out to the West Coast to introduce ourselves to e-commerce La La land. We met our new colleagues who all walked around in blue jeans and seemed to have computers permanently attached to their hands.

I was made SVP of knowledge development and started trying to figure out how to capture and grow our different disciplines. I liked some of the people in the individual firms. They were imaginative thinkers and were already exploring what digital marketing might become. But all of this was, of course, a house of cards. There was no real intention of combining all these talents and experience. We all sat around talking about value propositions and how we could deliver our combined capabilities, but all we produced were "sad stories of the death of kings."

A few months went by. Then in December, I was back in New York when I got a call from the chairman. He asked if I could come out to the coast the next week.

"I was planning to go to Anguilla."

"Can you cancel? It's important."

When I arrived, I was told we were way under our projected revenues. The fantasy wasn't coming true. The solution was to sell the firm again, and we had a buyer. He and his team were coming in a few days. His company sold software to mid-size retailers in the Midwest. On paper, he was worth a billion. Headquarters was in Chicago. It made a lot of sense, didn't it? Two days later, I was sitting next to Bob Bernard and he was explaining his vision of the new company. We were going to combine... We started the whole drill again. I was made SVP of knowledge development.

I actually liked Bob. He was in his mid-40s. His team in Chicago was loyal to him and had good Midwest values. He had a wife and two beautiful children. But with this deal, he surrounded himself with strangers, including me. The transaction was concluded on March 1 and the new company was named March First. That's not a typo. By that time, I could sell my stock because we had effectively sold MMG twice. I did. All of it. By the end of the year, a major crash in e-commerce had commenced and the stock became almost worthless.

A few years later, Bob died. I think it was heart issues. He was a good man.

So my first few years after McKinsey were quite a roller coaster ride. I learned a lot. At times, I felt like Nick Carraway in the *Great Gatsby*. Underneath the glamour of new technology, there was a great deal of crookedness. For a brief time, I quadrupled my income. But I was glad when it was over.

Republic Steel built all the houses in Indianola in the late '20s.
That's ours in the right foreground.

The tipple of the Indianola mine. It was torn down
a few years before I went off to Andover.

Ex-P-G Newsboy Wins Harvard Scholarship

William L. Matassoni Jr., 18, a former Post-Gazette carrier boy, has continued an outstanding academic career with such brilliance that he has been awarded a Harvard College National Scholarship.

Matassoni, of 6 Chest Drive, Indianola, now is a senior at Phillips Andover Academy, Andover, Mass., and his most recent scholarship, with a $2,800 stipend, admits him to the class of 1968 in the College of Harvard University.

Won P-G Scholarship

He has been attending the academy for the last two years on a scholarship he won in the Post-Gazette carrier boy scholarship program. He was selected for that honor from a group of 100 carriers interviewed by officials of the preparatory school.

He completed his sophomore year at Fox Chapel Area High School, where he was a straight "A" student in his studies for what he plans to be a career in science.

During his junior and senior years at Phillips Andover, his classroom diligence has consistently earned a place on the first Honor Roll and ranking in the first fifth of his class.

Highest Harvard Award

The National Scholarship, awarded in recognition of exceptional intellectual promise and strength of character and personality, is the highest honor Harvard College confers on incoming freshmen.

W. L. MATASSONI
More scholastic honors.

50 students holding this award in a class of 1,200.

The scholarships stipends are calculated to be sufficient so that the student can pursue his studies without employment or borrowing.

Top scholars of Andover's class of '64. I'm top right.

Newspaper boy makes good!

Photo of one of my Andover reunions. My best guess is it is the 15th, or 1979. That's George and Laura Bush on the mid-left; I'm on the mid-right, without a date.

My mother and I
at a family event.

Arriving with mom on Christmas Eve.

Playing soccer in Vail, Colorado in the early '70s.

Road trip in an old Mercedes coupe.

Style is attitude, and a pair of
cheap goofy sunglasses.

Bruce Nelson and I at one of our New
York loft parties. You either have it or
you don't.

On the terrace at my loft in Chelsea,
probably around 1988.

I can't remember the date or game, but it must have been the Steelers.

My goodbye lunch at United Way. That's the great Mario Pellegrini on my left.

Slim and I in a photo booth.
Young and crazy in love.
Probably in the late '80s.

Relaxing in Anguilla.

Tokyo, cherry blossoms and you know who.

We didn't change the design of Philip's house. Just the glass. Six tons became twelve. It was a bet that his concept could be made to work.

We replaced every piece of glass in our Philip Johnson house, almost by hand.

The living room was turned into a workshop.

"Nespoli," the sculpture we commissioned from Charles Perry,
being "delivered." Two tons of solid bronze.

At our little house
in Orient.

We had a 21' Boston Whaler on Long Island. Great fun.
Never, never used it for fishing.

Pamela in the kitchen
of our antique (1730)
house in the village of
Orient, Long Island.

Pamela with Ken Ohmae and me at the Savoy in London.
She was wearing heels.

Pamela and I got to know Dan Rooney, owner of the Pittsburgh Steelers.
One of the classiest NFL owners.

Pamela at a little seaside bar in the Keys. With a margarita in a 32 ounce mason jar.

Pamela. She was always the center of attention, except for me.

Pamela on the beach in Islamorada, the Florida Keys. Great legs, big feet.

10

THE BOSTON
CONSULTING
GROUP

h ERACLITUS WROTE that you can't step in the same stream twice. I knew that. Yet, a few years after leaving McKinsey and wandering around in e-commerce, I decided to take that second step. I accepted an offer to join the Boston Consulting Group as a partner.

The job was to co-lead a unit called the IMC, which stood for Innovation, Marketing and Communications. It was the brainchild of Carl Stern, BCG's CEO, and George Stalk, a senior partner who wrote a seminal management book entitled *Competing Against Time*. The objective of the IMC was to accelerate the creation of new ideas and move them faster from inception to client work. The concept was working, sort of, except BCG felt it was still playing second fiddle to McKinsey—and it was.

There were some problems I could see pretty quickly. Marketing for BCG still meant big, published ideas. BCG's lead partners believed that was McKinsey's strategy and decided to emulate it. Almost half the people in the IMC were editors and writers. There were no strong marketers in the group and no one really knew how to handle the press. The idea of actually owning an issue was foreign. More fundamentally, there was no theory or framework for innovation. The partners had very different views about how exactly to find new ideas and develop them. But I joined BCG because I had a lot of respect for them. They were a strong competitor to McKinsey. They were in the insight/chaos quadrant of the strategy consulting matrix I described in Chapter 2, a space I thought I knew well. BCG was the reason McKinsey had hired me.

I was ambivalent about joining BCG given how close I had been to McKinsey, Marvin Bower and so many of the partners. But time had passed and I had, in fact, been pushed out. Moreover, there were no secrets about McKinsey I could have told BCG that would have made any real difference to their competitiveness, largely because the two firms were so different.

I realized that for the first time when I saw a video of Bruce Henderson, BCG's founder. I couldn't believe how dissimilar Bruce was from Marvin Bower. Bruce was a salesman and an engineer (Vanderbilt). He wanted to fix the world. Marvin was a lawyer. He wanted to create a profession (consulting). Bruce thought in terms of systems dynamics. Marvin thought in terms of policies and principles. Bruce gave BCG a hunger for big ideas such as the experience curve and the four-box matrix for corporate strategy. Marvin, on the other hand, used to say, "At the top, there are no rules." He used to talk about the "arts" of management. For him, there was only the "integrated perspective" of the CEO. BCG developed its thinking in training sessions involving the entire consulting staff. It would write and rewrite short essays called Perspectives, which it shared with clients and target clients whom it would invite to exclusive seminars. McKinsey did things one on one. It wrote personal letters and cultivated relationships. It enjoyed taking its clients to dinner. And as for big ideas, Fred Gluck used to say, "Let a thousand flowers bloom."

So even though BCG and McKinsey were in the same market-space, their DNA was entirely different and so was the look and feel of the two places. For example, at McKinsey, compensation and advancement were determined by committees of partners who looked at several metrics, some hard and some quite soft. The engineer in Henderson distrusted those soft metrics. And he worried that committees get political (and there were times at McKinsey when they did). So, BCG's system was basically about one metric—revenue per partner. It had a culture of credit and everyone got measured the same way, whereas McKinsey had a culture of contribution. It was committed to measuring the soft stuff. For example, the members of the personnel committees would regularly stop by to see me to talk about the value of an idea or article. Was it new, did it attract clients, did it yield real insight and suggest new strategic options? It wasn't easy, but they cared. They cared about mentoring as well and asked pointed questions. They cared about the quality of our relationships with clients' senior management. The committees would personally visit client CEOs and ask questions about how many people from outside the local McKinsey office were brought in to the work because of the relevance of their experience or knowledge. By the mid-'80s, during Ron Daniel's fourth term as managing partner, revenues were a secondary factor—honest.

Not surprisingly, there was a lot of internal competition at BCG over revenue credits. There were inter-office rivalries that bordered on being unprofessional. And there were also many negotiations among partners to game the system. The revenues of individual offices received too much attention and were an impediment to moving consultants around to form the best teams for clients. But there were real friendships too. The partners loved to tell stories about great analyses at clients and they bonded over it. It could be a Jekyll and Hyde place, particularly for someone like me from McKinsey. I kept recalling to myself how Ron Daniel and Fred Gluck as managing partners once or twice a year would write a note to all partners highlighting new engagements where collaboration had made a difference in winning new work. They named the partners who had teamed up and cited the ideas that had made a difference. That culture was what BCG, and now I, was competing against.

I thought hard, of course, about how to position BCG against the dimensions of the strategy space and, in particular, how it was different from McKinsey. BCG could not come close to competing on the leadership dimension. It produced some notable CEOs but nothing compared to McKinsey. Its alumni network was weaker. You could argue it was smarter than McKinsey on the insight dimension but not so much smarter that it made any real difference when we were competing against each other. Some senior managers, the people who hired the top firms, might be more conceptual than others and might favor BCG, but the bloom was off the big idea. By the mid-'90s, management books had become a dime a dozen and many of the gurus had proved to be hucksters. I thought there might be another dimension where BCG had an advantage that had to do with competitiveness and winning. BCG was fond of the phrase "breaking compromises." They wanted more for their clients than bottom-line improvement. They looked for breakthroughs. I helped George write a book called *Hardball* that argued for a rough and "unfair" approach to strategy. It was a relatively successful book, but the partners never saw how it strengthened BCG's position or brand.

Trust was a dimension we also explored. Carl championed an idea that BCG's defining logic was insight, impact and trust. Trust is the opposite of playing hardball, but George and I thought they might go together. Sort of "me and Julio down by the school yard." Could you trust your consultant to push you hard yet respect your organization and its top management? McKinsey was trusted. Bain was not because of bad press about some of its clients where they were perceived to have pushed people around or replaced them. But trust is a tricky dimension. I once asked Ron Daniel if McKinsey served the company or the CEO. Ron didn't really answer and did not want to get into the issue. We serve both, he said. But we had positioned ourselves as a leadership factory. The answer seemed clear to me and gave BCG the chance to claim it served the company, not just someone's career. Fine, but which position on the trust dimension gets you clients?

BCG was regarded as apolitical and well intentioned. George and I promoted a couple of books to strengthen BCG's reputation for trustworthiness and the ability to translate trust into meaningful changes. One was entitled *The Change Monster* by Jeanne Duck; another was *The Forgotten Half of Change* by Luc de Brabandere.

BCG's strategy practice was run by a German partner, Bolko von Oettinger. He was more like Fred Gluck than Bruce. He could entertain lots of ideas. He introduced me to spatial strategy, the tenets of which influenced my thinking on marketing. In several ways, he was a Renaissance man. He liked art and gave me a wonderful lithograph for Christmas one year. Sadly, he lost his wife to cancer shortly after I met him. When he asked me to help him on his idea about strategic insight coming from poetry, I said yes. To me, it was a way of humanizing BCG. The project resulted in a book. I wondered if there was more we could do. We came up with the idea of a Christmas card. We asked some of our colleagues to read and record poems that were related to the holidays. The readings were surprisingly good and seemed sincere. We sent them to clients in emails and on discs. The recipients seemed to like them. I sent my "cards" with a note pointing out a couple of the poems. Believe it or not, I got a response rate over 30 percent. It was different and it was human.

We also tried to change the tone and voice of BCG. BCG had always sounded tough with its precise, simply structured prose. George and I tried to amplify that so authors sounded more like Hemingway or Spillane. For example, George came up with some terrific thinking about how to succeed at turning around a modestly successful organization. But it was a list. A smart list but just a list. I decided to give it context and entitled it "The Turnaround Man's Last Speech." Here's how it came out.

THE TURNAROUND MAN'S LAST SPEECH

Thank you for coming to my retirement party. I really enjoyed some of your cards and emails. A couple of them were even funny. Here's one: "You did a great job, you heartless creep." This one is good, too: "I never liked you, but I'm going to miss you." That was from my secretary. My mother wrote: "Just don't visit more often. I don't want my house reorganized again."

OK, I'll admit it. I'm a pretty single-minded guy. But when I arrived here three years ago, things were not good. You thought they were good, but they weren't. This company looked like it was profitable and growing. What I saw was complacency. And next to losing money, complacency worries me most.

In particular, the people sitting in this room, the top team, were not worrying about heart-of-the-matter issues—those few issues that will make or break the future of a company. Instead of focusing on what really mattered, many of our meetings—and there were lots of meetings—were dominated by minutiae, especially about good-hygiene accounting and corporate governance. Many of your subordinates were off attending seminars on empowerment and "managing your career like it was a business." Some of you even found time to get to New York to hear Jack Welch talk management to 600 of his closest friends.

To get your attention, I declared that the company needed to be turned around—despite its success. If we didn't do this on our own, sooner or later someone would force us to—by finding a better way to compete with us. Or another company would buy us and unlock the value we either didn't see or were sitting on.

Turning around a sick company is hard enough. Turning around a successful one is much harder. At a successful company, leadership doesn't have the luxury of losing money, which takes care of a lot of excuses for not changing. At an unsuccessful company, the first order of business is to stop supporting the things that lose money: unprofitable products and struggling stores. Boom! Profits go up, and you're a hero.

At a successful company, things aren't as straightforward. The key to turning around a successful company is finding the areas of competitive advantage and driving trains, planes and automobiles through them. You must push that advantage to ever-greater heights, even to the point at which other companies may complain.

What's more, at a successful company, it's harder to keep a turnaround going than to start one. At least five rules are required. If you, my friends, were not focused on these five rules, you were not on my management team. You were not, as far as I was concerned, earning your paycheck. So let's start at the beginning with the first rule.

All Investments Must Be Fast, Focused and Fundamental

If you recall, we had some rules for the investments we decided were key to turning us around. Every project we undertook had a market-demonstrated payback of 12 to 18 months. If it didn't, we broke it up until its pieces did. No multi-year investments in things like customer relationship management before payback. This is fast.

The trouble is that every on-target performance-improvement project attracts "neighbors" that really aren't fast or that slow down what needs to be fast. These must be rejected ruthlessly. This is focus.

And focus is needed because managers who are in turnaround mode can afford to spend time only on those efforts that strike at the heart of the matter. This is fundamental.

I know some of you thought my "3F" sweatshirts were hokey. So be it. I liked them, and I didn't mind the jokes. Keep 'em: you'll need them for when you're leading a turnaround.

Don't Let People Raise Obstacles to Change
Unless They Also Propose Solutions

What I did mind were the people who did not get onboard. It was not a time for nuance. That's why I insisted on rule number two. Nobody, as far as I am concerned, should be allowed to bring up a problem facing a turnaround without also offering options for bypassing the problem. Naysayers are a drag on and sometimes the death of successful turnarounds. That's why some people who started out with us are not at this dinner party.

Many companies concentrate on finding the right people. It is just as important, sometimes more so, to get rid of the wrong ones.

Most of you should remember my third rule.

Say Yes or No, but Never Say Maybe

I believe that the greatest stress on any organization is unclear direction. It's very easy for well-intentioned leadership to let questionable initiatives continue in the hope that they will generate something positive.

It is also easy to avoid conflict by letting people do things they shouldn't. Not good. The "three-legged horses" have to be shot. I said yes, or I said no. I never said maybe.

But give me a break. I didn't rule out changing my mind if new or better information legitimately allowed me to revisit an issue.

Most important, I didn't permit scarce corporate resources to be tied up on efforts that were not part of the agenda.

The fourth rule is the one I believe in the most, even though I wish it weren't necessary.

Keep Your People–Employees, Customers, Suppliers and Financiers–Informed

You guys know how sick and tired I got talking to "key stakeholders" about what the turnaround meant. But when I was most weary of talking, I knew we were only halfway there. People need to hear the logic for what is happening several times more often than may seem reasonable. When one of you gets my job, I invite you to ask some third- or fourth-level employees what they think the company's strategy is.

And then there's the last rule.

Leaders Do Not Get More Than One Chance

We have turned ourselves around. But not all of us have survived the journey. I know that some of you differ with me, but I believe that one of the greatest threats to a successful turnaround is keeping the people who do not deliver anything except excuses. I have been around management for a long time. I've seen many turnarounds fail because a key player was unable to deliver once, twice or even three times.

Leaders–and that's all of you–cannot allow this kind of slack. Time is too precious to tolerate even one failure to perform. This tightened tolerance needs to be made clear from the outset, and there must be "casualties." Colonel John R. Boyd, who headed the U.S. Air Force's Fighter Weapons School for many years, was famous for criticizing a top Air Force officer in Europe for having a low training-casualty rate. It was an indication, Boyd said, that the pilots were not being pushed hard enough. Not a nice message, but one that certainly makes you stop and think.

We were in a turnaround. We "survived" and prospered. Our competitors moved out of our way. You will be in a turnaround again. Sooner, I suspect, than you think. Let's remember what we learned.

Now let the champagne flow!

George Stalk Jr.

The response was quite strong. We kept pushing the Spillane voice. Our IT practice developed an idea about cumulative cash curves that was, they thought, a better way to look at investments than other perspectives such as "break-even" analysis. We turned that idea into an episode at an airport lounge. Picture a tired guy on his way home after spending the whole week in product development meetings. He orders a bourbon at the bar. At first, he doesn't notice the attractive woman on the next stool. Then he starts talking to her about how tough it is to make judgments consistently about different projects. She turns to him and explains the idea of cumulative cash curves. How you need to look at when and how long it takes the curve to turn positive and total input exceeds total output. Judge each project against that metric, she says. There is, of course, a bit of innuendo in the encounter. As he turns to leave to catch his flight, she looks over her shoulder and purrs, "Keep your eyes on those curves." I wish I had kept the first version. We tamed it down before publishing it, but it still got lots of comments and attention.

George and I tried other ways to get our partners to think about BCG's voice. Some of it was packaging. For almost two decades, BCG's primary vehicle for delivering its ideas was its Perspectives— short (800- to 1,000-word) essays that could fit into an executive's jacket pocket and be read on a plane. Still a good idea. But we started extolling the idea of "coffee-stained communications." Instead of a perfect piece of prose, we said, send something, maybe a couple of charts, that is wrinkled with notes on it and maybe a question or two in the margins. Something that would start a conversation rather than end it. In another attempt to get people to think about voice, we showed movie clips to the executive committee. We showed them the battlefield speech in *Patton*, brilliantly delivered by George C. Scott, and contrasted that with Sean Connery in *The Untouchables* asking Kevin Costner "What are you prepared to do?" We showed them Butch and Sundance at the top of the cliff before they jump. We hoped the clips would demonstrate that we had options in terms of our tone and style. They didn't work.

To be truthful, books and recordings weren't really going to be enough to advance BCG to a differentiable spot on some dimension of trust or humility. How do you do that for a bunch of partners who don't like having dinner with their clients? I thought there was only one way. You get them systematically to spend more unscripted time with those clients.

I found one senior partner who did. His name was Rich Lesser. He managed BCG's relationship with Pfizer, a relationship BCG shared with McKinsey. There were two dozen BCG partners on the Pfizer team. Rich assigned each of them to different members of Pfizer's top management ranks. He made sure that they each knew who last met with whom at Pfizer, what was discussed, and what might have been discussed. Rich regularly asked if BCG was being helpful—not selling, just being helpful. Were we building rapport? Trust? Admittedly, it was mechanical, but it was a practical and effective way for BCG to avoid getting out-lunched by McKinsey. I predicted that someday Rich and his team would earn the whole relationship. And, when Pfizer made a major acquisition, that's exactly what happened. BCG was asked to run the entire post-merger effort. I promoted Rich and his approach to client development at partner conferences. But not enough teams bought into it. The culture wasn't ready. It couldn't change twice.

Not many years later, Rich was elected BCG's managing partner. He was seen as someone who knew how to build client relationships—not the way McKinsey does but the way BCG could. I liked him personally because he was from Pittsburgh. He loved the Steelers. My old friend Joe Browne helped him get Super Bowl tickets.

I spent five and a half years at BCG. Just as at McKinsey, I enjoyed some great and productive friendships. Some notable publications and ideas resulted. But that wasn't the real game. George and I failed to gain acceptance of a new model for innovation. We argued that it was time to abandon Bruce Henderson's model. We felt that ideas were better developed inside the heads of smart associates or young partners when they received exposure to a class of problems. Problems like pricing or supply chains. This to us was better than Henderson's time-honored debates at practice meetings among consultants who had one or two experiences with a problem. We failed because to get a consultant multiple exposures to the same issue or problem, BCG would have had to weaken offices' control over client assignments and strengthen it among practice leaders. For example, let's take this young guy in the Atlanta office who has done solid work on pricing for Delta and move him to Chicago to work on pricing in consumer goods. That would have accelerated innovation. Would Delta have liked it? Probably not, at least at first. Would the associate or young partner? Maybe. He or she would have had a chance to apply new ideas in new client situations and probably raise BCG's impact. The biggest impediment was it would have required changing the credit system for offices and individuals. And, as George said in his turnaround speech, that would have taken big-time commitment. We would have needed to evaluate practice leaders on their creation and contribution of world-class thought leaders, not publications or total revenues.

Without a major change like this, it was going to be difficult for BCG to own issues. I mean really own an issue the way Bain owned the concept of "loyalty." Ironically, there was precedent. Early in his career, George demonstrated how to do it with his work on time-based competition. He moved himself and his family to Japan to immerse himself in the concept and it paid off for BCG. George didn't just write a book on time; he infected BCG with his thinking. He did the same thing with e-commerce where BCG took a big lead over McKinsey.

On the topic of pricing, George narrowed the issues down to pricing innovation—ideas that could help a company change the basis of competition and all the decision rules. For example, in work it did for GE, BCG developed an approach for pricing locomotives that focused on "power by the hour" rather than horsepower per se. George also championed some first-rate thinking on port congestion to position BCG against the broader issue of supply chain management. He got significant press coverage for his research. But to no avail. BCG was not willing to invest in idea development the way we saw it. It was easier to hire editors and dress up ideas for publication than use the staffing process to create young, world-class experts who knew how to apply their ideas in client work. Ironically, the IMC had one of the biggest discretionary budgets at BCG. Money wasn't the problem. It was behavior. Back to the challenge of social marketing.

I also failed to convince practice leaders to focus on value propositions rather than frameworks and methodologies. Professional service firms need to prove to potential clients that they will be worth their fees and deliver value. To do so, they often resort to value "proofs." As I noted earlier, these proofs are usually examples of their past work. Or they detail methodologies—XYZ named processes—that guarantee good results. Both can work, but over the years I had come to believe that a more effective approach to convincing clients that your firm can really help them is to develop compelling value propositions.

There is a rigor and logic to strong value propositions. First, they contain a definition of the problem or opportunity. It can be concrete or abstract—managing a global supply chain, for example, or leading an organizational turnaround. Convincing value propositions start with three or four insights about the situation. What spells success or leads to failure? What is counterintuitive? Second, a good value proposition describes the managerial challenges that result from your basic beliefs regarding success and failure. It lays out what leaders need to do to win and what they must solve for. This may seem straightforward, but often it's not. If your basic beliefs contain both durable and new insights, they can help managers see better what confronts them and assess whether they are ready.

Having defined managerial challenges, a good value proposition then needs to address a basic question in an honest but not arrogant way. Why an outsider? Why can't management address these challenges on its own? What information, perspective, resolve, etc. is missing? And finally, a strong value proposition needs to answer one last question: why us? If an outsider is needed, why is it you? What people, skills and knowledge—that's all professional firms have—make you a clear choice among your competitors? And how does that relate to the one dimension in your space where you are king. Good value propositions define the problem in your terms.

BCG had about 25 industry and functional practices. I could not get around to enough of them to put momentum behind the idea that their goal was expertise between the ears of young consultants and clear value propositions that our consultants used confidently. So I failed to do what I was brought in to do—make the IMC unit work to integrate innovation, marketing and communication. But I really liked working with George. He was smart and he was fun. We both liked bourbon. He was a great partner. We trusted each other even though we were as different as Bruce and Marvin. We were Butch and Sundance. He insisted on facts; I always asked for examples. He was a scientist; I was a storyteller. I recently told him about this book and its theme of selling ephemeral things. He said immediately, "Don't forget that ephemeral things are what help you raise prices. Functionality can help you get only so far. It's that ephemeral stuff on top that gets you the premium." Vintage George.

Carl tried to give us as much backing as he could, but he had a lot on his plate trying to steer BCG through a steep downturn in the global economy. He decided not to stand again for CEO and then George and I were outmanned. There was something else too. About halfway through our effort at running the IMC, George got very ill. He went into a coma for several weeks. It got so bad that Carl asked me to write an obituary for him. I took over the IMC unit and did as well as I could. George, because of his tenaciousness and courage and love for his family, pulled through. But we never got our momentum back. So after five years, I stepped out of the stream once again. That said, George and I remain best friends.

11

MARKETING IS SYSTEMS REDESIGN

S O THERE I WAS in my mid-60s wondering what next. Or if there was going to be a next. Should I retire to our mid-century modern house in Connecticut? Or spend more time on the north fork of Long Island in our little 1730 house on Orient Harbor? Make more use of the Boston Whaler that sat at the yacht club most of the summer? Or was there still more to learn and do?

I wasn't sure. I wasn't really a marketing expert. I was a guy who lived a lot of marketing. On a whim, I took over as CEO of a consulting firm in Boston that advised family-owned businesses—huge companies actually. Most of their consulting was pattern recognition and hand-holding, but the partners were professional and served their clients well. There was not much of a strategic perspective in their work, which was a big hole, so I convinced George Stalk to come in as a partner and fill that gap. It worked out because George, with his experience and age, related well to the founders of the firm's clients. He could talk about strategy without a bunch of slides in his hands.

But the firm really didn't need a CEO so I decided to leave. I took on a couple of consulting assignments. Manpower hired me to give them advice about their market position. They were losing share in their markets, which were largely about filling administrative positions.

They had, of course, already explored the idea of helping their clients recruit more educated or skilled and higher-priced individuals—kind of an obvious dimension that needed to be explored. But it was basically a product extension and their competitors were already exploring it. Putting on my dimension cap, I started to think about a spectrum that ran from individuals to corporations. Where was the power in Manpower's revenue model? Well, it was with their corporate clients. That's where their fees came from. But maybe the world was changing a little and individuals were gaining more power, particularly in the ranks of the skilled—programmers, sales, etc. I suggested that Manpower become Mypower.

Why not empower the people you are recruiting? How? For one, help them form communities where they can learn from each other. Say you're a mid-level employee of a four-star hotel in Berlin. Wouldn't you like to be able to talk to others in your position at other hotels around the world? What do you need to do to get ahead? What might you get paid if you do? What might lie five years down the road for you? The idea did not go anywhere. There was a lot to figure out, for example, a whole new revenue model. Would current clients go for it? Could it work in some segments alongside the old model? Could Manpower, now Mypower, actually deliver the technical, functional and emotional benefits to its new customers so they felt they could control their destinies? Manpower was a well-run company with a good senior team, but the change monster was firmly ensconced at its Midwest headquarters. So my assignment ended. Nevertheless, I enjoyed the work and it encouraged me to keep thinking about dimensions that were truly different.

Around this time, Bill Novelli called and asked me to serve on a strategy advisory committee for the AARP. Bill had taken over as CEO of AARP and had two objectives. First, make it a more powerful voice on policies that mattered to AARP members. Second, make its for-profit arm bigger and more profitable. As usual, he was taking an aggressive approach to both goals and he was succeeding. For a couple of years, I shuttled to Washington each quarter for an afternoon meeting with Bill and about eight other members of the committee, including Newt Gingrich, followed by dinner. The discussions were lively and we had some impact on Bill's thinking. So much so, it seems, that AARP's board became worried about our influence and asked Bill to disband us. Too bad. It was fun spending time with my old friend.

Then I got a call from Tom Woodard, a friend and partner at McKinsey. We were close. When we were there, he ran the electronics practice worldwide for McKinsey. He was very capable. A Baker Scholar and a great team builder. And he certainly knew how to have fun anywhere in the world. There was that time at Villa d'Este.... After retiring from McKinsey, Tom had taken a senior position at a firm called Tapestry Networks. I had not talked much to him recently even though he and his wife lived nearby in New Canaan. He asked me if I would be interested in a consulting assignment. I said I don't know. The pool was set at 89 degrees and it was a great place to smoke cigars. He sent me some material on Tapestry and what it did for its clients.

It seemed to me that Tapestry's basic business involved building and sustaining "networks" of people who had a corporate board function—for example, head of the audit committee. They would meet at nice places and discuss issues they confronted in their role as board members. Were they all worried about cybersecurity, for example? Was customer privacy becoming a more difficult challenge? Typically, there were about 15 members of each network. Meetings would include dinner the night before followed by an all-day discussion. Tapestry's people would facilitate these meetings and write up extensive notes. The notes were dense but well done and well received.

Many of Tapestry's people had legal backgrounds. Lots of policy and regulatory issues would come up and be captured in the notes, but there was no effort made to change either. That was for the members to do individually. Tapestry explicitly stated that it did not lobby.

The networks were paid for by corporate sponsors (it was a sophisticated way to meet potential clients and gain substantive knowledge about changing issues) or by the members themselves. The model was quite profitable, but in recent years revenues had been flat.

I read the reports and thought they were all pretty much the same and that "progress," however defined, was not rapid. Then I read about what was called the European Healthcare Network. It was a brave new world for Tapestry. It began when one of the network members asked Tapestry to take things further, to actually try to change things. He was on several boards but also the head of the European operations of a major pharmaceutical firm. He told George Goldsmith, Tapestry's CEO and founder, that his company was very frustrated with its investment in drug development. It would take years and millions of research dollars to get a new drug approved by EU regulators and a price set, but even then, that wasn't enough. In Europe, each country buys drugs for its citizens. They don't have to buy what the EU approves. In many cases, they would reject an "approved" drug, saying it may be better than the drug it could replace, but not that much better to justify the increase in price.

"Couldn't Tapestry help us on this? Otherwise, there are going to be fewer and fewer new drugs in the pipeline and everyone will lose."

"Tapestry," he said, "is good at getting friends—people in the same role—in the room. Can they get enemies in the same room? Can it get them to see the problem from different perspectives? To see the problem as a systems failure."

And that is what Tapestry did. But it wasn't easy.

In Europe, regulators are very cautious about communicating with the private sector. They certainly are not encouraged to. They regulate companies but don't talk to them. What happened is remarkable. The work is described on Tapestry's website (www.tapestrynetworks. com). It took Tapestry a year just to get the different players—the drug researchers, the payors, the patient advocates, etc.—to agree to meet. In those first meetings, there was little candor and even less understanding of how the drug development system was failing and how continued failure would lead to poor health for millions of people—all because people were doing their job.

But in the next year, enough trust was established so that the stakeholders were willing to explain how they saw the world and how others were failing. As a result, perspectives changed. The drug approval process was then examined with a much more dispassionate view and questions arose about what information and what evidence was actually useful in uncovering the potential success and value of a new drug. It started to become clear that hundreds of millions of dollars could be saved for each drug in the pipeline. And how, if those dollars could be saved, prices could be lowered and yet the drug companies could still meet their investment goals.

In the third year, a redesigned drug approval process was piloted for all the drugs the participating drug companies were working on to treat type 2 diabetes and breast cancer. The results were non-binding, but the pilots were a success. They are now being used to change the system for drug development in Europe. Key to this progress was a commitment by all the stakeholders to a common and higher goal—to get the right drugs to the right patients at the right price. That may not sound like a lofty mountain top, but it reminded all the players how much more value could be created—lives saved and healthier lives lived—if that goal could be reached.

The reports of the meetings Tapestry produced for this network read differently than the reports for their other clients. They probed and asked questions and in an informal way got the participants to check their assumptions about behavior and outcomes.

Then good things happened. Here's Forrester on the process:

"The most intense disagreements usually arise, not because of differences about underlying assumptions, but from different and incorrect intuitive solutions for the behavior implied by those assumptions. In building a system dynamics model, one starts from the structure and the decision-making rules in a system. Usually there is little debate about structure and the major considerations in decisions. When a model has been constructed from the accepted structure and policies, the behavior will often be unexpected. As the reasons for that behavior become understood, I have often seen extreme differences of opinion converge into agreement."

Tapestry, intuitively or accidentally, had drifted from facilitation into systems modeling.

So there we were, sitting around the pool, George, his wife Ekaterina, Tom and I, eating tuna salad and drinking a nice Alsatian pinot gris. George wanted Tapestry to grow and do more work like the work in European drug development. He detested the thought that clients tended to think of Tapestry as a facilitation firm. Could I help? I honestly didn't know. Should Tapestry move into a new space? What were its dimensions? Even if Tapestry did not lobby, could it, in fact, influence the policy and the social systems those policies affected? Did it have the right people to do the work? Could it sell its new role to clients, both old and new?

I liked George. He had spent several years at McKinsey so we spoke the same language. He was a genuine serial entrepreneur and very engaging. We admired the same people such as Jay Forrester, the MIT professor who is often credited with inventing systems dynamics. It would be great to work with Tom again, who was basically George's right-hand man and mentor. We agreed to an exploratory one-month assignment—an assessment of Tapestry's market position.

I spent two years at Tapestry, off and on, both as a consultant and as a member of their senior management, trying to shift their role from facilitator to systems redesigner. Once again, I underestimated how hard it is to turn around a company, particularly when things aren't broken—recall George Stalk's Perspective.

I remember early on at a meeting of Tapestry's partners I put up a chart, a "from-to" chart and suggested that Tapestry needed to move from "left to right." Instead of getting peers in a room, we needed to get "enemies" in the room. Instead of static summaries, we needed to work on dynamic models, etc. The older partners didn't like it. "That's not what we do." The younger partners did. One of them went with me to visit with Earl Sasser, formerly a professor at HBS who was now running Babson's MBA program. He was skeptical. "You are not going to get your partners to move from left to right. And you probably are not going to get your clients to do so." We would need to find new people and new clients.

He may have been right. My friend Mark Leiter, who was then head of strategy at Nielsen, arranged for Tom and me to meet with its vice chairman. We had a nice discussion with her about privacy and whether Nielsen and a few of its big customers, Disney for example, should form a network around the issues of privacy. I think we intrigued them, but it didn't go anywhere. I also had a connection with Atlantic Philanthropies. They were winding down their operations but wondered how to bring their work to an end. They were particularly interested in palliative care. I floated the idea that they form a network with others that would, in a sense, "outlive" their grants. I tried to hook them up with Bill Novelli and the work he was doing at

Georgetown on end-of-life care. We labeled the dimension we were trying to sell as "governance and leadership." Our clients were going to advance society's ability to deal with complex problems. It was a hard sell. Harder than I expected.

My experience at Tapestry made me ask myself if my simple theories about dimension and market-space were sufficiently robust. In the early '80s when Ken Ohmae wrote his book on strategy, *The Mind of the Strategist*, he portrayed a marketplace with three circles, which he labeled company, customer and competitor. There were only winners and losers, who were determined by the interactions of these players. Ken's dominant theme was creating and sustaining competitive advantage.

But Ken knew better. He knew there were other players and stakeholders involved. He was, after all, a graduate of Waseda University in Japan, with a degree in nuclear physics. He worked on the first fast breeder reactor at Hitachi. So, he knew something about how complex systems worked. He would have readily granted that in industries such as pharmaceuticals and energy, there are other important players in a market: regulators, policy makers, insurance companies, etc. He also knew that how they interacted with each other and the outcomes can be pretty hard to predict.

So, I needed to ask myself, and now you, gentle reader, if the basic idea I've been advancing–that marketing's primary task is to create new dimensions in a market-space–is still relevant and useful in highly complex industries and environments. I believe it is, but it needs to be reshaped. First, the market-space itself must be thought of as a dynamic system, not just a multidimensional matrix. Second, dimensions themselves may be better defined as superordinate goals that the various stakeholders need to embrace and see as consistent with their goals. Looking back on my work with the National High Blood Pressure Education program, I realize that's what we were doing when we shifted the focus from detection to compliance. That caused everyone involved to see their job differently. The new goal didn't ask any of the stakeholders to be saints by focusing on compliance. The pharma companies could still try to sell their drugs to doctors and regulators who could still focus on ensuring the safety and effectiveness of the drugs, but the new goal changed their behavior so that the system as a whole created more value. More people took more drugs and kept their blood pressure under control, thereby saving the country millions of dollars in healthcare costs.

The key was a superordinate goal that helped people see that they were involved in a system in which win-win was just as possible as win-lose. The Nobel prize winner John Nash, in fact, proved that win-win outcomes are more likely than win-lose outcomes, but it is hard for participants in a market to see this or to make it real. At best, they see ways to compromise and find common ground. But they rarely see the opportunity for higher ground.

An example: One of the biggest threats to our health and welfare in the U.S. is the scarcity of drugs to treat Alzheimer's disease. The increasing number of older people in the country is making the problem worse. We know this and have known it for a while. Yet, there have been only three new Alzheimer's drugs approved in recent years by the FDA. Why? Because the system that connects drug companies, regulators, patients, payors and physicians doesn't work very well. It costs hundreds of millions of dollars and takes several years to create a drug and get it approved. Because of time lags and lack of metrics, cause and effect are harder to define. So is value. What is a drug worth over what period of time for what population of patients/consumers? To understand this system requires study and communication. Perceived enemies need to meet and eventually trust each other. Goals need to be found that get players to work together. Those goals often look like the new dimensions of value I have been describing. They change the game for everyone and they make win-win more possible. I believe that marketers—not regulators, policy experts, insurers or patient advocates—can make Nash's theory a reality and add tremendous value to society.

What we learned, or at least what I learned, from Tapestry's work on drug development is that new dimensions or superordinate goals are born of contradictions. A goal of getting the right drug to the right patient at the right time and price is filled with contradictions and conflicts. Getting new drugs to patients takes development speed but may sacrifice safety. In BCG's words, these compromises need to be broken and they can be with pricing innovations (price the drug according to its effectiveness over time, for example) and other systemic changes. The new goal and the resultant system changes redirect participants' behavior so they both give more and get more and everyone gets the piece they want of a bigger pie.

Back to our theme of marketing ephemeral things. This is not fluff. This is real value. Real value for multiple players at once. The way to prosper and make progress is to give and to get at once. Exchange but not compromise.

So, I have come to believe that there is a new role for marketing to play in a world of seemingly intractable problems—problems in healthcare, education, the environment, privacy and other areas. I believe marketers can do a better job against these challenges than policy makers, regulators and other players. By "do a better job," I mean they can help competing parties create more value for themselves and others. Both economic and social value. They can do this not by finding compromises that satisfy different players, common ground, but by instead finding higher ground. Dare I say it is a new paradigm—a big shared idea. And I believe they can do this using an approach that is similar to what I described earlier as searching for new dimensions of value. By keeping everyone's eyes focused on the right goal. Whereas the formula used to be create, communicate and capture value, in multi-stakeholder markets it becomes create, capture and share more value.

Tapestry, to my mind, had bent the drug development space; it had grabbed the system by its shoulders and said, "Look what you're doing and look how you are failing." Ironically, Tapestry itself is now torn about what it really is. It is very good at high-level facilitation. It is just learning about how to advance society's ability to govern and lead—a new mission I asked them to consider. It will take new kinds of people—not lawyers, policy wonks and scribes alone. It will take people who know how to understand a system, scientists and space benders who can find new ways to assemble levels, flows, policies and decisions. And it will take the new kind of marketer I have been describing.

The jury is out. A professor at HBS, Karthik Ramanna, wrote a case about Tapestry working with George and me. I am not sure it has been taught yet, but I am sure the students will be skeptical of an organization whose goal is to "advance society's ability to govern and lead." Tapestry is currently doing some very promising work on Alzheimer's and palliative care. The woman leading this effort, Lindee Goh, is a physician. She was a successful consultant at BCG. Her network is now taking a system-based approach to multi-stakeholder problems that our modern, aging society needs to address such as palliative care. I introduced her to my old friend Bill Novelli, who now teaches at Georgetown, and they are looking for ways to work together to address a topic that some people are afraid to discuss. Who will pay for system changes that ensure that people get to die the way they want to die? AARP? Maybe, but its many members will certainly not agree on what it means to die the way you want to and, in the process, save yourself and the country millions of dollars. Again, it won't be easy to find the new policies that will make things better for people approaching the end of their lives. But I am confident Lindee and Bill could lead an effective and gutsy effort.

Two other young partners from Tapestry, Nicholas Gertler and Mathew Diver, have launched out on their own and found clients to demonstrate the value that a combination of systems design and marketing can create. I stay in touch with them. They have described to me their work for a big pharma company that wants to get into antibiotics.

The challenge is that current healthcare systems make it very difficult to make any money in antibiotics. Nicholas and Mathew were asked to evaluate incentive policies that had been proposed. They discovered rather quickly that the proposals were all vague. One of the key themes emerging from their work is that large organizations are themselves multi-stakeholder entities. It is very difficult for them to go beyond generalizations when they engage externally. Nicholas asks, "Who speaks for a $200 billion company? In an area like drug development, distinct parts of the organization are responsible for distinct and technically complex aspects of the medicine's life cycle. They all operate under the assumption that the system stays as is."

According to Nicholas, to make sensible proposals for improving the system, the companies need to clarify internally where they are and where they want to go. "This calls for an iterative dialogue to surface objectives and pain points, develop concrete proposals to address them, and evaluate those proposals from the perspective of the various functions. All this, says Nicholas, before you go outside."

So the various management theorists who talk glibly about building "ecosystems" should respect the need for self knowledge. "For example, you may find yourself in a situation where the regulatory requirements are shifting innovation in a therapeutic area. To get something to change, you need to put forth some concrete and credible proposals. But what to propose? Any changes must address patient need, make clinical trials faster and more patient friendly and lead to a drug that is commercially viable. All while ensuring that medicines are effective and safe." Nicholas says he and Matt and the client team locked themselves up in a room for several days and came up with 11 distinct designs for how antibiotic developers could be rewarded without encouraging over-use of their products. "And then we tested each of these designs for how well it worked with the medicines in the companies' pipeline. The winners were the proposals that the company took forward."

The new marketing profession I am calling for has no room for vagueness or glibness. Who will these new professionals be? What will they look like? Well, they will look more like Matt and Nicholas than a "graduate" of P&G. Yes, they will have all the tools of segmentation and pricing and strong analytical capabilities. They will need to start with the same basic checklist McKinsey published in a staff paper in 1988:

1. Benefits explicit, specific, clearly stated.

2. Price explicitly stated.

3. Target customer clearly identified.

4. Clear how this value proposition is superior for target segment.

5. Evidence of adequate demand.

6. Evidence of acceptable returns.

7. Viable in light of competitors' value propositions.

8. Achievable with feasible changes in current business system.

9. The best of several value propositions considered.

10. Clear and simple.

But they will have new tools as well to help them solve simultaneously for both dimension and design. They will at least have the basics of systems dynamics in their repertoire. Systems themselves can be very complex, but the basic analyses that are required can often be put on the back of an envelope. New-age marketers don't need to be computer programmers, but they will need to do a little modeling and read primers like Donella Meadows classic, *Thinking in Systems*, that will help them get a better understanding of how system constraints once released can lead to abundances and back to constraints. And why certain rules of systems redesign (it's better to dampen a reinforcing loop than strengthen a dampening loop) make sense. They will think imaginatively about where to deliver information and feedback in a system where it did not exist before. In Meadows' words, they will replace classic market tests and learn to dance:

"Magical leverage points are not easily accessible, even if we know where they are and which directions to push on them. There are no cheap tickets to mastery. You have to work hard at it, whether that means rigorously analyzing a system or rigorously casting off your own paradigms and throwing yourself into the humility of not knowing. In the end, it seems that mastery has less to do with pushing leverage points than it does with strategically, profoundly, madly letting go and dancing with the systems."

They will also have some experience with social and regulatory policy as both Matt and Nicholas do. They will need to have worked in places like Washington and Brussels and have a feel for the sausage-making process of policy. Most importantly, they will have empathy—the ability to put themselves into the shoes of others. I don't mean compassion or advocacy. I mean the ability to stand outside the glass wall and look in. (As Meadows says, "We change paradigms by building a model which takes us outside the system and forces us to see the whole.")

I guess we all go out with a whimper and not a bang, but it's nice to have various ideas you have admired and collected come together for you as you reach the end of your career. And still keep learning. My experience at Tapestry rounded out ideas I had discovered at Ashoka, 30 years earlier. More about that in the next chapter.

12

THE MODERN
SOCIAL MARKETER

SO WE COME CLOSER to the end of this memoir—an account of my journey from a coal-mining town in Western Pennsylvania through Andover and Harvard, and then McKinsey and BCG—a journey that took me all over the developed world. I have been exposed to lots of ideas, mostly about business and management, not politics or social science. That said, over the years I have come to believe that markets and marketing, more than policies that aim to protect and restrict, can make the world work better. My definition of marketing (as I suggested in the last chapter) is pretty expansive, including, as it does, systems redesign.

Looking back on things, I realize now that my career at McKinsey shaped my understanding of strategy and marketing. Part of it was figuring out how to improve McKinsey's standing, how to make it an institution that was sui generis. And part of it was figuring out how to give our ideas currency and relevance. But a big part of it had nothing to do with consulting. It had to do with meeting and working with Bill Drayton, a McKinsey alum who founded an organization called Ashoka and helped mightily to start a movement now known as social enterprise.

Drayton and Ashoka introduced me to people who were changing the world, often in big ways. These people were all social entrepreneurs.

You won't often read about them in the newspaper and they won't be on the *Today Show*, but they will make a big difference to us all.

I met Jimmy Wales, the founder of Wikipedia, only once, but it was a memorable encounter. Jimmy is a great example of a social entrepreneur. He saw a problem—unequal access to knowledge—and he set out to fix it. He set out to make all the knowledge in the world available to all the people on earth in all the languages we use. Has he succeeded? No, but he is a lot closer than when he started. I was at a conference sponsored by Ashoka that featured several social entrepreneurs. One of the breakouts included Wales and Wikipedia. I attended and listened intently to Jimmy. During the Q&A, I asked him if he was interested in somehow monetizing the information Wikipedia was collecting on trends in people's interest and information needs. He basically said no.

"Nope, my goal is to get all the knowledge to all the people. Until I do, nothing much is going to distract me and us."

I thought to myself, wow, that's commitment and purpose. I'm not sure I agree with Jimmy because I would rather see Wikipedia be more self-reliant financially, but Pamela and I are happy to make a donation each year because of the success of its model and its effectiveness.

Drayton created Ashoka about 40 years ago. He did it with money he got when he won the MacArthur Prize, which is often called the "genius award." And, yes, he probably is one.

Ashoka's slogan is "innovators for the public." Bill believes that almost any social problem—in education, healthcare, the environment, you name it—can be successfully addressed by imaginative and determined people who dedicate their lives to developing new markets and systems. Ashoka funds these entrepreneurs with small stipends to cover just their living expenses so they can pursue their ideas full-time. There are almost 4,000 Ashoka Fellows and they are changing the world.

For example, one South American Fellow noticed that in his country, the best students did not get into the best schools. They lacked both money and access. He decided to change the system by which their education was financed, using an idea that Milton Friedman had proposed decades earlier. Instead of loaning money to students, he offered potential investors a share of their future earnings. So, the more money they made in the future, the more their investors made; and the less, the less the investors earned. Not surprising, now that the best students had the funds to enroll, they did quite well after graduation and so did the investors who bet on them. Those schools that regularly produced successful students became the most attractive to investors. They were happy with their returns and the students were happy with the fees they paid. Much better, they realized, than paying off enormous student loans. This new approach has now spread to other countries in South America and elsewhere, even the U.S. where government-backed student loans dominate.

Notice that bankers were not involved in this effort. Lacking imagination, they did not see the opportunity to provide investment opportunities to their clients. All they could see were student loans—a lousy business. The financial sector is pretty weak when it comes to progress obtained through social innovation. Much the same can be said of government. That's why we need what Drayton calls the "citizen sector."

One of the major trends in marketing in recent years has been strategic plans based on drastic cost reduction. In several cases, market structure has been altered by social entrepreneurs and philanthropic organizations seeking to serve what has been labeled "bottom of the pyramid" segments. But if you look at these cases carefully, they are much more than drastic cost reduction or even new technology and business models. They are about systems redesign. Several years ago, I became a trustee of First Book, an organization dedicated to getting books into the hands and heads of poor children whose parents could not afford to buy them a book. There are millions of children in the U.S. who grow up in homes where there is not a single book. You can imagine the effects on children in these homes in terms of literacy and eventual livelihood.

Over the course of 20 years, First Book has managed to distribute 160 million books to poor children. Along the way, it has changed the way the children's book market works and greatly expanded that market because of the price reductions it has engineered. Drayton puts it this way: they have not only provided people fish and taught them how to fish; they have changed the fishing industry.

First Book started off its efforts basically begging for books and storage space. Publishers worked on a consignment basis. If the books didn't sell, they got them back. So, they ended up with lots of unsold books in their warehouses. First Book offered to take them off their hands. To distribute the books, First Book contacted people who work with children and recognize how important it is for a child to be able to read and write: teachers, of course, community organizations, etc. They discovered that there was considerable demand. They charged a small fee to cover their shipping costs.

After a few years, the two founders, Kyle Zimmer and Jane Robinson, realized that logistics needed to be much better if they were to reach a goal they set for themselves: 1 billion books. They set up the First Book National Book Bank, a warehousing system that took advantage of unused capacity to distribute college textbooks. They also beefed up their "retailers," adding thousands of people who were motivated to get the books and pass them along to poor children. This phase of their growth was vital because they began to aggregate demand and that gave them power. They could be helpful to publishers by taking large amounts of unsold books off their hands. But that was only phase 2.

In phase 3, a whole new business model began to take shape when First Book's leaders realized how the book publishing business worked and where value got created and lost. With their aggregated demand, they could now say to publishers we will buy, not take on consignment but buy, this many thousands of books. We will pay you around $2 per book. Why would the publishers agree to sell books for $2 that they might sell for $22 at a fancy bookshop? Because it was a sure deal. Their cost of making another book was very modest. But they needed to be sure none of these books were sold into their higher-priced channels and cannibalized their sales. First Book could guarantee them that would not happen through its newly created First Book Marketplace. First Book's business model thereby changed. It was no longer a not-for-profit distributing free books. It was a wholesaler selling books into a rapidly expanding network of agents. They became "sustainable" in the sense that their operations just about broke even. They have found that there is big demand for books at $3 per copy, much more than at $22. Moreover, they could specify books that were best sellers with children, not just the leftovers. And they could have a voice in creating new books that appealed to minorities in poor communities.

Why do I tell you this story? Because I admire First Book and respect their willingness to attack the root cause of an oppressing problem in our country—illiteracy. Just getting a book into a home isn't enough, but it is a first and vital step. I also tell the story because First Book's leaders represent the new breed of marketers we see emerging who can work among different players to create a new system and market structure that is profitable and creates value for several stakeholders at once. And I tell it because Kyle and Jane had the vision to wed both for-profit players and not-for-profit players into a value chain that successfully pursues both economic and social goals. What's neat is that a totally for-profit chain couldn't do what First Book does. It would not have access to the market segments First Book members can reach—all those teachers and community organizations—with whom they have built a trusted brand.

Several years ago, I helped Bill Drayton write an article for the Harvard Business Review on the "citizen sector" and the role of "hybrid value chains." One of the examples was First Book. Another was a building supply firm, Colceramica, that was able to open up the low end of its market by teaming up with community organizations similar to those in First Book's model. The combination of players developed a new pricing scheme that allowed customers to buy products on terms they could afford. Colceramica's brand was strengthened at the same time its revenues and profits grew. Other players in the housing market—governments and policy makers—were happy because the housing supply was increased. So were retailers, insurers, etc. A win-win through systems redesign and pricing innovation in a market that is estimated to be worth over $400 billion.

Ashoka has many entrepreneurs working in healthcare. One of my favorite examples is a for-profit hybrid that includes private businesses, venture capital and citizen sector non-profits. It's called E Health Points and delivers healthcare to rural villages in India. It uses video technology and electronic medical records so that patients don't have to travel and sacrifice income to reach a doctor. Its clinics keep costs low for patients with a combination of advanced point-of-care diagnostics, generic drugs and careful local staffing. Consultations cost $1. The clinics also provide clean water. It's working. The players are reaching their goals and making enough money to be sustainable and grow. Models like this can be exported to many countries, including developed ones.

Ashoka is now using its scale to learn from the work of its fellows. It encourages its fellows to communicate to each other what they are discovering and to formulate what it calls "mosaics" of successful new approaches. For example, about 90 of them are addressing the problem of mental illness and it's clear that what they are doing is changing society's impression of what mental illness is and then changing the systems used to "treat" it. Society, they conclude, must see mental illness as much more common than rare. It must see mentally ill people as capable of helping themselves and becoming independent. That care is not just medicine but a new system that includes peers and local organizations. These entrepreneurs see how their task is to change perception as much as it is to change reality.

Clearly, there is an overlap between the work of my former Tapestry colleagues, Nicholas and Matt, addressing multi-stakeholder problems such as drug development and the value chain invention of social entrepreneurs like Kyle and Jane. They are true modern marketers bringing together multiple players by getting them to see and measure value differently. They don't ask these players to be saints. They ask them to be smart and understand each other and respect each other's goals.

I've been a fan of social entrepreneurs like Kyle and Jane ever since I met Drayton back in the early '80s. Things get changed for the better when an entrepreneur recreates a system with new and old stakeholders. In many cases, government is less involved, although new policies are necessary to help the entrepreneur make the reconceived market work. But the new policies are simpler (limits to the percentage of earnings investors get, for example). Social entrepreneurs are the new marketers. What they do is entirely different from corporate social responsibility, sustainable sourcing, etc. Social entrepreneurs create systems that work more for everyone by changing policies and decision making. They ask the right questions. In a school system, for example, are there alternatives to funding from local property taxes? Must salaries be the result of tenure?

It may seem overreaching to argue that marketing can fix our underperforming school systems, but bear in mind that school systems are, in fact, systems with levels, flows, policies and decisions. If we see evidence that marketing can fix multi-stakeholder systems such as drug development, then let's conclude that it can fix education by getting people to debate what matters: the goals of the system, how participants get rewarded, etc., rather than complaining about funding and other factors that have been found to have relatively little influence on results. A judge in a recent Connecticut court case on school funding called for a "radical reimagining" of our schools. To me, that means we need to find the new dimensions that drive players in school systems toward the sustained behavior, call it compliance, we want and need. Politicians are not going to do this for us. Nor are teachers and unions. Not without marketing, as I hope it can work, at the center making sense out of nonsense. Or, as Jane Austen might say, finding the truth from contradictions.

Now, if you are game, rewrite the above paragraph and put in housing instead of education. You can almost leave the rest of the words the same. Time and again, low-cost housing policies and projects have failed. Systems design experts have shown why they fail. But instead of reimagining with others how they might work, we settle for patchwork answers such as putting "poor entrances" on the sides of luxury buildings where we demand that a certain percentage of apartments be rented to low- or mid-income residents. It is pathetic and corrupt to talk about a housing "market" when this kind of thinking is tolerated.

If you are really game, rewrite the above paragraph and put in healthcare. I got an essay from Fred Gluck the other day; its perspective is almost entirely one of systems redesign. Before he joined McKinsey, Fred was the program manager for the Spartan anti-ICBM missile system at Bell Labs. He wrote, "All these excessive costs have been well documented and commented on for many years, but the political will to face the problem, consolidate the insurance industry, reduce complexity and transition to integrated delivery systems has been lacking. This is not surprising given the clout of the vested interests of not only the insurance companies but also all the other institutions, think tanks and experts that have made a career of refining a flawed system, not to mention the number of unproductive administrative jobs that will have to disappear. However, there is no way to reverse the spiraling costs of care without addressing these fundamental flaws."

Markets get corrupted. Costs get added that don't add value directly to the product or service. High taxes, unnecessary additives and ingredients, etc. can all be considered corruptions, no matter the justification. Monopolies corrupt markets when they prevent competition based on price and merit. At the extreme, criminals and extortion corrupt markets. For many of Ashoka's social entrepreneurs, the task is to take corruption out of the world's markets. They believe they can do this in three ways. One of them, and this should not surprise you, is transparency. George Stalk frequently asks what will happen when the cost of bandwidth goes to zero. More specifically, "What if you could have any information you want, in any form you need it in, anywhere, at any time at zero cost?" Well, some good things can happen if you put the bandwidth and transparency in the hands of a young man in Nigeria determined to prevent deaths from counterfeit drugs. He developed a cell phone-based verification system that works remarkably well for all the participants—patients, pharmaceutical companies, regulators and phone companies. The percentage of dangerous fake drugs in Nigeria has dropped rapidly.

Markets also get corrupted when a product or service is scarce and price is not used to allocate it. I told you the story of how an Ashoka entrepreneur solved this problem in his country by linking student's interests with the interests of schools and investors. His idea of "human capital contracts" is taking off and will likely make a big difference to the financing of education. A third way to stop the corruption of markets is just good old-fashioned courage. Entrepreneurs in southern Italy, part of a farm cooperative, showed a lot of it when they convinced merchants and consumers to band together against the Mafia's extortion of their distribution and stores. Merchants agreed to display a sign that promised they would not pay off the Mafia anymore and urging consumers to buy from only them. It sounds idealistic and only one gunshot away from failure, but it has worked! Free markets are, it seems, much more powerful than we think against fearful enemies. So maybe the goal for a new breed of marketers is restoring integrity to markets by ridding them of corruption.

Maybe the biggest cause of market corruption is good intentions. One of the brightest young associates I worked with at McKinsey, Amar Bhide, wrote an article for HBR in 1994 entitled "Efficient Markets, Deficient Governance." It details all the efforts we have made in the U.S. since the Depression to protect investors. He argues that we may have succeeded in some ways, but we simultaneously traded informed shareholders for arm's-length diffused stockholding. As a result, CEOs complain that investors are fixated on quarterly earnings, while investors see many CEOs as entrenched, overpaid and self-serving. He points out the direction we need to go. "Good governance requires real policy trade-offs. Clever tinkering with insider-trading and disclosure laws cannot get around the basic conflict between market liquidity—which requires transient, arm's-length shareholding—and close honest shareholder-manager relationships." Trust ultimately is the key and our regulations have weakened trust. Politicians are not going to help. We need Ashokans and system redesigners who keep their eyes on the prize by developing policies that increase the levels and flows of trust.

Don't get me wrong. Not all young people considering marketing as a career need to think about saving the world. Great-looking lingerie and nutritional beer could be fine places for them to apply their talents. Or they can lead the way in developing new commercial markets such as mobile power. Besides bandwidth, there are several forces—demographics, globalization, security, urbanization, deconstruction—that will demand dramatically new approaches. But the sky's the limit for people with brains and guts, and Ashoka's exemplary people are proof.

Recreating multi-stakeholder systems requires defeating those who just want their share. They should want more. The challenge is to make them see more and see how to get it. That's marketers' new role in society. It was Drayton—as soft-spoken, determined and well-intentioned a man as I have ever met—who over the years gave me the conceptual framework that helped me understand that marketing strategy is more than connecting Ken Ohmae's customers, competitors and companies. Marketing is about defeating the people in charge. About defeating the people who would keep an industry unchanged, who would write policy that limits prices and competition—timid, unimaginative participants who insist that the customer is always right. It was Drayton, all 135 pounds of him, who helped me understand that marketing is about creating new systems that house new markets that explore new dimensions that create new value.

Back to poetry and artistic expression one last time. In an interview in the Paris Review, Ralph Ellison reportedly said, "I recognize no dichotomy between art and protest." Echoing Ellison, Harvard PhD candidate Clint Smith says, "Part of what it means to be an artist is to imagine the world as it could be." Recall Ackoff's definition of strategy: "the active synthetic skill of designing a desirable future and inventing ways of bringing it about." Poets, strategists, marketers all—that is the challenge.

Bill Drayton believes everyone can be a changemaker. You too. Marketers come in all ages and stripes. Consider your next career.

***

Thank you for reading my memoir. Lest I close on too serious a note, let me offer one last thought...about beer. It is an excerpt from a review of a book that tells the history of beer.

"*Ancient Brews* may well get readers drinking (in moderation, of course). It will also get them thinking, especially when Mr. McGovern ponders alcohol's place in human society. Fermented beverages didn't just provide our ancestors with a good buzz; they 'tapped into the hidden realms of the human psyche.' For the ancient world, drinking 'contributed to a joyful exhilaration in being alive, much like the congenial atmosphere of today's neighborhood bar or a shared meal or celebration.' Civilizations may rise and fall, but as long as humans walk the earth, they will do so with mug in hand."

13

IDEAS AND PEOPLE

Pamela Valentine. My wife of 30 years. She still looks like a model with the same great legs she had when I met her. The dimensions of our private market-space have changed a little, but she still seems crazy about me and I am still nuts about her. Also known as Slim, Slimbo and the full Slimbowski.

Anna Laczek Matassoni. She was a devoted mother and loved my father despite his drinking. She pushed me out of our little coal-mining town. She made me take a test that resulted in full scholarships to both Andover and Exeter. A year later, I was admitted to Harvard. Without her love, foresight and courage, my life would have been very different.

David Honick and Jim Morris. My mother was the force in my life. David and Jim were vital early influencers. David was a distant relative, a kind Jewish man who taught at Lesley College in Cambridge. When my Greyhound bus arrived in Boston, he picked me up and drove me to Andover. For the next few years, he was my local father. I spent holiday weekends with him and his wife in Cohasset when I could not afford to go home to Pittsburgh. When I told him I was thinking about applying to Oberlin, he said nonsense. "You are going to graduate at the top of your class. You are going to Harvard." Similarly, Jim Morris led me to my first job in sales after Harvard. I was coaching the varsity soccer team at Colorado Academy. We won the state championship my third year. He came up to me after the game and asked, "Now that you have done this, isn't it time for you to make some money?" I asked him what I should do. He said, "Go sell stocks and bonds." I told him I didn't know the difference between a stock and a bond. He laughed. "You'll figure it out." So, after spending the summer in London courtesy of a fellowship from the English-Speaking Union, I went to the local office of Bache & Co. The manager, Lou Germano, said, "Let me get this straight. You delivered newspapers when you were a kid, you're Italian and you graduated from Harvard. You're hired." I knew nothing about stocks, but bonds were just math. Within a year, I was running the bond department at Bache and driving a nice Mercedes. GNMAs and FNMAs had become my friends. If you are very lucky, people like David and Jim show up in your life and point you where you need to go.

Marvin Bower. Bower was an inspiration to me. Above all, he taught me that you need to understand your values before you try to live them. The picture at the end of this book was taken at one of Marvin's birthday parties.

Samuel Beckett. I graduated second in my class from Andover and won the math prize. When I got down to Harvard in the fall, I majored in mathematics and astronomy. I took a course on "multi-dimensional function spaces" that I really enjoyed. So the concept of dimension in this book is not casual or metaphorical. Thinking about the dimensions of market-spaces defined in Cartesian or other ways can be rigorous and quantitative. But it is still better to be roughly right rather than precisely wrong when thinking about how fast and how much a new dimension will emerge.

By senior year at Harvard, I had turned my attention to the humanities and wrote a modest undergraduate thesis on Samuel Beckett. I learned that Beckett studied mathematics before he turned to literature. My thesis focused on the mathematical themes in his novels and plays. How he tried to permute and combine words in the hopes that some meaning would pop out. How irrational numbers and asymptotes showed up in several ways and informed his view of life and consciousness. Beckett's back-against-the-wall humor had a lot of math in it.

Four years earlier, one of my teachers at Andover, **Dudley Fitts**, had prepared me for Beckett. Fitts taught an honors class for seniors. I would come in off the playing fields on a fall afternoon, cold, wet and muddy, take a shower and join about a dozen of my classmates in a small basement room of Bullfinch Hall (circa 1818) to find Fitts in a wheelchair at his desk. He was never late. We sat around him and he read to us. He read Greek tragedies he himself had translated. And then he read T.S. Eliot–"Wasteland," "The Four Quartets," "Sweeney Agonistes." One day, he read Eliot's critical essay on Cowley, a metaphysical poet. The essay asked if modern man can think and feel at the same time. When I read Beckett, it reminded me of this question. Essential contradictions, qualitative vs. quantitative, the different ends of dimensions. These themes stuck with me and survived the dull curriculum of business school.

Early in my career at McKinsey, I read Donald Schoen's *The Reflective Practitioner*. Among other things, the book describes the interactions that take place between the problem solver and the problem. Schoen's definition of strategy is now my definition, or at least hope, of what marketing could be: "The active synthetic skill of designing a desirable future and inventing ways of bringing it about."

Jay Forrester is considered the inventor of system dynamics. There are a lot of smart people in the world who still think statically rather than dynamically. They think they can change one variable or one relationship in a system and that the rest will remain unchanged. We get lots of very bad policy from static thinking. And bad marketing too. As I have said in this memoir, if you want to be a great marketer, a true systems changer, you need to study systems design. MIT has a MOOG if you are interested. Forrester, who no doubt is right, believed you will need to do a little systems dynamics modeling (*Learning through System Dynamics as Preparation for the 21st Century*, July 2009). Forrester actually believed that man could answer Eliot's question positively. He wrote in the paper I just cited that "Transferability of structure and behavior should create a bridge between science and the humanities. Feedback loop structures are common in both. An understanding of systems creates a common language. Science, economics and human behavior rest on the same kinds of dynamic structures. I see a reversal of the trend toward specialization. As the underlying unity between fields becomes teachable, we can move back toward the concept of the 'Renaissance Man,' who has broad intellectual interests and is accomplished in areas of both the arts and the sciences."

Bill Drayton, the founder of Ashoka and my friend for over 40 years, showed me the relationship between social entrepreneurship and systems redesign. Social entrepreneurs reinvent market-spaces. Bill walks his talk. He takes one vacation a year, a solitary hiking trip in the mountains, lives modestly and pays himself little, and devotes all his waking time to pursuing his goal of turning us all into "change-makers."

If I was lucky in my early career to meet Drayton, I was just as lucky to meet **Bill Novelli**. He gave me my first real job after HBS at Porter Novelli. He was a great boss. He was tough. He played tailback at Penn and he wasn't that big. We played soccer together in an amateur league in Maryland. On the field, I could take chances at halfback because I knew he was behind me, ready to clean up my mistakes. After the games, we would raid his kitchen refrigerator and eat bologna sandwiches. Bill left Porter Novelli to run the Campaign for Tobacco-Free Kids. He kicked ass and took names and won. Over the eight years he was CEO of the AARP, he made it a much bigger and more powerful force for social change. He is now teaching at Georgetown University where he heads the business school's work on social enterprise and marketing. He is also leading an effort to change the way our social and healthcare systems address palliative and end-of-life care (C-TAC). Like the other people listed here, he is the kind of guy who leaves his mark on you.

George Stalk at BCG, like Bill Novelli, believed a good strategy demolishes the competition to the point they cry "unfair." As I said in Chapter 7, George was a great partner for me at BCG because we were so different from each other. He favored bourbon over Bordeaux, evidence over example, charts over concepts. He embodied the spirit of BCG and its pursuit of what really matters in business.

Ken Ohmae: Brilliant. I don't use the word often, but Ohmae was hands-down brilliant. I was very lucky to meet him at McKinsey and to work with him all over the world. We had some good times together in Tokyo. Ken was key to the efforts we made to make McKinsey an institution that people saw as unique.

And so was **Carter Bales**, who was the inspiration for our efforts to position McKinsey as a leadership factory. Carter passed away recently. The list of people who consider him to have been a friend and mentor is long.

Fred Gluck, McKinsey's managing partner in the mid-years of my career there. He gave me the assignments at McKinsey that helped me grow, for example, building a system to capture and share our knowledge and experience. Fred and I worked together intensively on these projects. His instincts were rarely wrong. We had a lot of fun together.

Another McKinsey partner, **Warren Cannon**, managed me during my first few years at McKinsey and made sure I was properly presented as a partner candidate. In subtle and not-so-subtle ways, he taught me how partners of prestigious firms should behave and how confidence, resolve and humility should fit together. When I had brain surgery, he sat with my family for nine hours as they awaited the outcome.

Ron Daniel, McKinsey's managing partner when I joined in 1980, has always for me been a total class act. When he led McKinsey, he truly understood and lived the concept of a "servant leader."

Tom Peters. Whatever I said in this memoir about working with people who want to break the rules and change things applies 10 times to Tom. A true wild man. He gave me a plaque that still hangs on my office wall. It reads, "Dr. Fame."

Michael Silverstein was my Tom Peters at BCG. Again, a rule breaker.

Alan Kantrow, **Brook Manville**, **Partha Bose** and **Stuart Flack**. I brought them all into McKinsey to do important work; they all delivered and all of them made partner. I am proud of that.

Bill Price, **Janet Santoiema**, **Joanne Ferrari** and **Susan Bergel**. Before the Internet and email, people called you. Someone picked up the phone and said, "This is Bill Matassoni's office." Over 20 years at McKinsey, these four people did that. They made me sound responsive, articulate and kind. They were not there to "protect the boss." They stood on the outside of my little glass house and reminded me that I was best when I was actually helping people.

Tom Steiner, founding partner of Mitchell Madison. When I left McKinsey, one guy reached out to me and said come aboard. You're the man we need. Tom gave me the opportunity to prove myself outside McKinsey. I will always be grateful to him for that.

Mario Pellegrini. Larger than life, the man in the big leather coat. Mario lured me away from Porter Novelli to work with him at United Way. The work we did together on the NFL campaign was one of my great adventures.

Joe Browne. Joe was my counterpart at the NFL for that campaign. Later in my career, whenever I had a complicated press or public relations challenge, I called Joe. He has great instincts. We have remained good friends and it has nothing to do with the fact that he always got Super Bowl tickets for my family when I asked.

Bruce Nelson. He became head of creative at McCann-Erickson at 30. Thirty years later, he finished as vice chair of Omnicom. Like Joe, my best source of advice and counsel for decades. The protagonist of many, many "what happens in Vegas" adventures. His insight and enthusiasm were infectious. He embodied the kind of unique talent that New York City attracts.

Philip Johnson. I never studied architecture, so I can't say that the discipline of architecture has instructed me. But it has inspired me to think about marketing as a spatial challenge. Most of this inspiration came from living in our wonderful house designed by Philip. He visited us several times after we bought it in the early '90s. On one of his visits, he said, "You realize that I was breaking up the Miesian cube when I designed your house?" Pamela and I looked at him and laughed, "Of course!" What he meant was his client, a wealthy French family, had asked him to build them a glass villa rather than a glass box. "At first," he said, "I didn't know how to do that, but then I figured it out." What he figured out was how to build a glass house where the walls did not divide inside and out. Philip was always encouraging and supportive when we asked him for advice. After he completed the visitors' center at his house, he asked us to come over and check it out. We enjoyed our time with him.

Charles Wick. I became a trustee in the late '80s of the U.S. Information Agency/Voice of America when it was run by Charles. Its purpose was to tell the world about America. That meant more than broadcasting news. What stories would it choose to tell? Charles believed the duty of the agency was to reveal the character of Americans and the principles of American life. I was a bystander, but the experience was very instructive to someone like me who had little insight into the ways of Washington. Because of my involvement, I got to introduce Pamela to President Ronald and First Lady Nancy Reagan at a State Department dinner in Washington.

Michael Boricki, partner of FIRMSconsulting. I have to mention Michael and **Kris Safarova**, another talented partner of FIRMSconsulting, for two reasons. First, I would not have written this memoir had he not encouraged me to do a series of videos about marketing and my career. Second, he gave me another great thought about beer. "Many people forget," he recently wrote, "that in ancient times everyone drank beer because the water was so bad. The fermentation process killed most of the bugs and made it safer than normal water. In other words, just about every great person from ancient times was slightly drunk when they did their best work." You can say that again.

Last, but certainly not least, my sister and brother, **Kathleen** and **David**. Despite my father's drinking, we were a happy family. We loved each other and still do. Kathleen gave my mother three grandchildren, whom she adored, and David made her laugh so hard she could barely breathe.

14

THERE MAY
BE HOPE

S INCE I FINISHED MY MEMOIR about a year ago, I have seen evidence that some of the things I wrote might be true. I realize that this could be, as the Rock Man said to Oblio, seeing what you want to see and hearing what you want to hear, but this is my story and I'm sticking with it.

HERE ARE SOME NOTES AND ARTICLES WORTH CONSIDERING

"St. Louis Wants Judges Thinking Beyond Cash Bail," Johanna Wald, April 5, 2019, Wall Street Journal

This article shocked me in that it described exactly the kind of systems redesign I've advocated. It recounts how a former New York City Detective, Wilford Pinkney, is "working with city officials to help establish processes for pretrial reform and, as part of this work, develop procedural alternatives judges can use in lieu of bail." It describes how Pinkney is "bringing in key stakeholders—judges, police, probation officers, defense attorneys and social workers—and breaking down silos so that people are not held in jail just because they can't make bail. Says one judge, this is not about being soft on crime. "Pinkney considers one of his biggest challenges to pretrial reform to be that of persuasion. He wants to convince stakeholders not to be constrained by the current system. "If you think about the walls and barriers and restraints as they currently are, you're going to limit your ability to think about what could or should happen, he says. I want stakeholders to consider what they want a system to be rather than assuming it has to stay the way it is. This can be a challenge for people but they have to dare to dream." If nothing else, enormous amounts of money can be saved by keeping people out of jail. I guess the big message from my memoir is we need a lot more Pinkneys in our world. He is a modern social marketer helping to find systems changes that translate into a world that works better.

That said, we can't underestimate the entrenched perspectives that the Pinkneys are up against. In my memoir I praised the efforts of an Ashoka fellow who is changing the way students are financed through income share arrangements (I.S.A). Instead of borrowing from the government, students borrow from investors and pay them back with a percentage of their future earnings. A recent article in the New York Times notes that "private investors have thus been...pushed to the margin of what has become the largest non-mortgage debt category in the United States; the federal government has over 90 percent of the market." The private I.S.A. sector has yet to reach 1 percent, but it's growing fast. Still, the Times writer warns of the dangers of this promising idea. "Welcome to the world of subprime children. This is the path we're on, and it ends with teenagers being careful to always smile in front of their laptop cameras lest the I.S.A. algorithm find them uninvestably dour. The alternative is to reconsider education as a social good and make capitalists pay for it, not as an investment but via taxation. If we're not careful, investors from Silicon Valley and beyond will reshape the country's children in their own image." I don't agree with the writer, but that's the kind of thinking marketers who seek to change our society's systems will face. ("What's Scarier Than

Student Loans? Welcome to the World of Subprime Children" May 11, 2011, New York Times, Malcolm Harris).

Working with Your Enemies

In the memoir I described how Tapestry, a consulting firm, helped define and develop a new approach to drug development in Europe. Nicholas Gertler, one of the consultants who worked on the assignment, recently told me that the new approach is working! Government agencies are collaborating with private sector companies and the costs of developing new drugs is coming down in Europe.The approach is now becoming the standard for approving and pricing new drugs. You could argue that it is just one case, but I choose to believe it is one more piece of evidence that there are huge opportunities to redesign systems and find win-wins. (See my discussion with Nicholas in the upcoming Season Three of *The Bill Matassoni Show*.) But we have to make sure we go beyond vague talk of inclusivity and free speech. Unfortunately in the U.S. we have increased our willingness to "fast-track" drugs, i.e. take shortcuts regarding their effectiveness, to get them to patients who might benefit from them. Why not fix the system rather than circumvent it? (Wall Street Journal, July 5, 2019, "Fast-Track Drug Approval, Designed for Emergencies, Is Now Routine").

Social Enterprises

I also described how social entrepreneurs are changing how we think about difficult issues in almost every area of our lives: the environment, healthcare, education, etc. The number of social entrepreneurs around the world continues to grow and the social enterprises they create make a real difference. They are changing policies in one country after another in every area they explore. They are attracting some of the best talent available. Increasingly, private sector companies are turning to them to be partners. That's where we will learn how to make society work better. I just got a note from Kyle Zimmer, head of First Book, that sales of books and educational resources on the First Book Marketplace exceeded $1 million in April. That's over $4.2 million retail. First Book has become a trusted brand for educators serving poor children.

If you have a chance, visit Ashoka's website and read what some of the fellows they recently funded are accomplishing with very modest resources. It will be clear to you how what they do differs from traditional philanthropy. They will lead the way in many areas where stalemate and lack of progress are now the norm. If you have time, visit two other sites. First, Hystra.com. It was founded by Olivier Kayser, a former McKinsey director. It helps its clients develop hybrid business models and new marketing approaches. It's first class in terms of its rigor and insight. The new businesses it helps create are both sustainable and profitable yet serve people at the very bottom of the economic pyramid. And take a look if you are curious at affordablehousinginstitute.org. It works all over the world with key actors in housing such as government, lenders and philanthropies. Systemic problems have plagued attempts by these different players to work together effectively, even in developed countries. AHI's founding CEO, David Smith, has brought approaches that work to break through barriers and build lasting homes for people who can't afford them.

Places to Spaces to Dimensions

I introduced in my memoir the idea of market-spaces as opposed to market places. I noted that market-spaces can be a strategic advance if they are created around a new dimension of product or service.

More and more I am seeing companies seeking and defining new dimensions in what seemed to be well established markets. I'm also seeing companies and their leaders recognizing that it is not enough to use new technology or develop a new business model. The model needs to deliver a new dimension. Otherwise it's just an improvement. Moreover, the conviction to deliver the new dimension has to be driven by a belief in yourself–a belief in your new self.

As I watch some of the competitive battles going on today, that framework–new technology/market forces leading to new business models leading to new dimensions leading to new identities–helps me sort through the various players in a market and who might win.

Take Netflix for example. Netflix's original business model in 1997 was based on both new and old technologies–personal computers and the U.S. mail. Then, in 2007, 10 years after it was founded, it discovered streaming. The success of YouTube convinced them they could deliver their movies and TV shows digitally. But that delivery system was not a new dimension. What became the new dimension for Netflix and for the space called home entertainment was time. Or better, timelessness. Netflix saw how much freedom it could give its customers. It saw how new patterns of consumption emerged in its ever bigger audience. It also learned how to interact with its customers to the point that 75 percent of what they watched was content Netflix recommended. It learned that the rules for packaging content could and should be changed. It started to ask why do segments of content need to be confined to 22 minutes. It also started to ask what if it released new series or seasons all at once. It asked how it could work with its suppliers of content to change the question of "When?" to the answer, "Whenever."

As I have read about Netflix recently, it seems it has discovered a new dimension and identity that is all about time, or the absence of time, and now sees itself not as the last link in a supply chain, like Apple, but as an orchestrator of an ever larger multi-stakeholder network. As an orchestrator, it will not necessarily set the rules, but it will make sure rules—rules about pricing, privacy and other issues—get set.

The Importance of Identity

I made a big deal in my memoir about the importance of identity. I described how McKinsey changed its identity from "preeminent management consultant" to "leadership factory." My point was strategists who seek to bend and expand their companies' market-space succeed or fail to the extent they change how their organizations see themselves.

My guess, and it is only that, is Netflix's emerging and strengthening sense of how it should operate with its partners will give it an advantage over new challengers such as ATT, Apple, Amazon and Disney +. It's an advantage that has little to do with whose installed base is bigger. Instead, it's rooted in its evolving sense of how to compete and collaborate.

Observers of the home entertainment streaming industry have noted that would-be competitors of Netflix will have to change their mission and identity. In early April, the Wall Street Journal ran an article with the headline, "To Battle Netflix, Disney Goes for the Big Remake: Itself." It contends that "One thing is already clear. The undertaking requires a whole new set of skills, and a major cultural shake-up. Disney must transform itself from a company in which every movie and theme-park ride it produced to perfection to a tech company capable of moving nimbly in a hypercompetitive space. ... 'done is not a thing in tech' said one longtime Disney employee who left last year. It's like oil and water. Two completely different management philosophies."

Ecosystems

The concept of multi-stakeholder networks figured prominently in the latter chapters of my memoir. I described how organizations from the public and private sectors might collaborate to not just share economic and social value but create more of it. And I opined that the discipline of system dynamics could help them do that. The top consulting firms are beginning to bring method and example to the concept. BCG in particular has led the way. Martin Reeves, who leads BCG's Henderson Institute, has co-authored two articles, "The Myths and Realities of Business Ecosystems" and "Getting Physical, The Rise of Hybrid Ecosystems." Every CEO and strategist should put them on their must-read list. I hope that BCG will follow up with a third article that pays more attention to the role nonprofits can play in these multi-stakeholder systems, how they get rewarded, and how the system dynamics work to keep all the participants focused on a superordinate goal. But hats off to Martin for solidifying BCG's thought leadership.

Capitalism

The Kindle version of my memoir made no mention of politics, although I made it clear that I am a believer in markets' ability to drive innovation and growth. Markets to me are the heart of capitalism. I did recommend on my reading list Joe Bower's book entitled *Capitalism at Risk*. Since the mid-term elections in the U.S., capitalism has been in the news. Some political leaders have advocated for a more restrained and regulated form of capitalism. Business leaders are taking up the cause of saving capitalism. Ray Daleo, for example, is publishing essays on "why and how capitalism needs to be refocused." He writes that American capitalism is not working for the majority of Americans and cites "low income growth, and ascendant income and educational failures." Other CEOs, Howard Schultz of Starbucks for example, are offering remedies for making society "more fair." So is Peter Georgescu, retired CEO of Young & Rubicam, in his latest book *Capitalists Arise!* Among the academics, Mike Porter is offering ideas on how to make democracy work better.

I still remember watching Fritz Lang's Metropolis for the first time. Is there a right version of capitalism? Most of the recent critics believe in capitalism and advocate collaboration between the public and private sector and more enlightened (read less greedy) leadership by CEOs. But if that means conferences and roundtables in Washington, don't get your hopes up. I wonder if we would be better off and make more progress in terms of improving the quality of people's lives if we addressed multi-stakeholder problems such as healthcare and the environment at a lower level of abstraction that focuses participants not on political philosophy but what I called in the memoir superordinate goals.

For example, one of the biggest problems facing the U.S. is the state of its infrastructure. Both major political parties say we need to repair and expand it. What does that mean? If we keep the debate at the level of political philosophy, the question will be who pays for it. But what is it? Is it filling potholes and expanding roads? BCG has advanced the goal of "access." The goal is not transportation, it says. It's better ways to get "there" and get things. It defines access as "the number of valued destinations that inhabitants can easily reach within their daily travel time budget." (*Solving the Cooperation Paradox in Urban Mobility*, November 2018).

Keeping pace with BCG, McKinsey has founded a research center focused on mobility that looks more broadly at the idea of "infrastructure." Aren't there better ways, it asks, to help people of various circumstances get healthcare, education, food, work? There are good reasons for hope, says McKinsey. Its research on "reimagining mobility" looks at cars, consumers, cities and competition and suggests many ways we can and should improve the country's infrastructure. Most of them have little to do with potholes. "Mobility is about to become cheaper, more convenient, a better experience, safer and cleaner—not 50 or even 25 years from now but perhaps within a dozen."

Obviously, it is going to take a lot of work, the right people involved, a much better and dynamic view of the problem, and the active guidance of the kind of marketing I advanced in the memoir. It is a much more daunting task than improving the bail system in our courts, but the same principles apply. And my hope is that the discussion and debate will inspire the kind of enlightened entrepreneurship and reinvention of systems we have seen accomplished by social entrepreneurs. One caution: as smart as my old friends at BCG and McKinsey are, they have a lot to learn about how to get both enemies and friends to work together. I'm not sure they can do that; there could be a big opportunity for new firms.

The Four Seasons

As I put the finishing touches on this memoir, I got the news that the famed New York City restaurant is closing. It was to me the ultimate market-space. Literally. It was designed by Philip Johnson and Mies van der Rohe. It was in part an immense glass cube, yes, very much like our house in New Canaan. We have reproductions of the bar stools in our pad in West Palm.

The Four Seasons brought several innovations over its 60 years, "farm to table" for example. But the unique dimension it brought to the world of restaurants was power. You didn't pay for the food. You paid for the presence of all those people who made things happen in New York and in the world. Publishers, writers, financiers, performers.

A meal was about power. A regular table was about ultimate power. Philip had one in the grill and was there often.

The Four Seasons lost its lease. It tried to move and recreate its magic. It didn't work. All good things come to an end.

Notre Dame

The fire that destroyed large sections of Notre Dame has given us a great challenge. Great in the sense of complex and important. How does France rebuild its monumental cathedral? Why does it rebuild it? What is the superordinate goal? To literally reconstruct it with old French oak? New French oak? Or steel? To what purpose? To enhance tourism? To reinvigorate Catholicism, which has lost 20 percent of its followers in the last few decades? Can the lessons learned from New York's rebuilding of the World Trade Center memorial be applied? What were they? Let's hope that the French people can put aside the debate about who pays and come to an agreement about a great goal that inspires everyone involved. (*France Debates a Modern Spire for Notre Dame*, Wall Street Journal, April 17, 2019)

The Role of Emotion

In May of this year, Michel Roux passed away. Roux turned Absolut, a little-known Swedish brand, into the top selling imported vodka in the United States. He did it by adding style and sophistication, starting with the bottle design. "I want to make a fashionable business out of the booze-peddler business," he once said in an interview. He targeted gay and lesbian consumers.

Like Victoria's Secret, he brought new and emotional dimensions to a market that was waiting for something to happen.

I should note that Victoria's Secret just announced it has cancelled its annual fashion show on network TV. That doesn't mean that the dimension of sexiness it introduced to the lingerie market was a failure or even that it's past its prime. It just means that times and channels change.

One of the movies I recommended was entitled *Her*. It's about a divorced man who has an affair of sorts with the operating system on his computer. More broadly, in the memoir I noted that emotion is playing a bigger and bigger role in product development. Technical, functional and emotional benefits and dimensions need to be skillfully blended and delivered. Then, a few weeks ago, I read an article that notes "As we seamlessly transition from screen-based interfaces to voice-first interactions, we have begun to identify the products we use in our daily lives by name instead of by brand. In turn, we are increasingly expecting not just utility and performance, but also trust and emotion. This fundamental change in behavior is forcing us to reimagine the possibilities of every product we build today." Told you so. (*From Design Thinking to Emotional Thinking: Designing Products with E.Q.* Syuzi Pakhchyan - Experience Design Director - BCG Digital Ventures, May 1, 2019) The article goes on to say that "For decades we have created digital tools to streamline our lives; now we must think of these tools as companions, coaches and advocates." It concludes that more and more "we must design products led by the heart." You know where I'm going with this. If marketing is going to save the world, it will do so by seizing our imagination and emotion. Whatever the challenge—restoring a cathedral, creating a new-age infrastructure, curing cancer, saving our planet—that's what it will take.

The Role of Leaders

A few months after the Kindle version of my memoir appeared, I heard from my former McKinsey colleague, Brook Manville. Brook now runs his own consulting firm and writes a blog on leadership for Forbes. com. He said he liked my memoir and wanted to write about its implications for leaders. We talked for an hour and a few months later his blog appeared. He entitled it "Why Reinventing Systems Beats Just Solving Problems." He tells his readers that my views on marketing are really about leadership. Whether you are the CMO, CSO or CEO, your job is to go beyond problem solving and be a systems designer. He closes with five propositions for today's leaders:

1. System change begins with systems thinking. Get familiar with the basics of information stocks and flows, feedback loops, intervention points, etc.

2. Humanize your systems thinking with intangible values too. Consider things like different stakeholders' sense of identity.

3. Harness action with superordinate goals. Bring marketing-style savvy to explain why overcoming this or that big challenge really matters to people.

4. Run experiments and keep learning. Systems reinvention must be an ongoing process.

5. Embrace the energy of capitalism. You need stakeholders around the table to fight each other. Avoid feel-good corporate social responsibility and beware of zero-sum games.

Just as he did at McKinsey, Brook makes my thinking better and summarizes it well. If you want to read the whole blog, go to Forbes. com and search for Brook Manville, Leadership Strategy.

Beer

How could I end this without mentioning beer again? I'm seeing evidence that my thought that a new and successful dimension of the beer market might be nutrition. That we might see some beer producers pitching products that are billed as being good for your health. A recent article in the Wall Street Journal ran with the headline, "Can Beer Help You Recover After Exercise?" The article reports "a new spread of low-cal, low-carb, even electrolyte-infused options are turning craft beer from reward into recovery drink. Once, recovery meant rest. Now it can seem as active as exercise itself." The article notes how many beer makers are getting into wellness beers, "There's definitely a trend to market craft beer to active people, and even some data that suggests that active people are drinking more."

That all said, there is still some confusion between the old low-cal dimension and the new good-for-you dimension. Most entrants will no doubt try to establish positions on both dimensions, but why not high-cal and wellness? You might have more credibility there, and heavier drinkers. Not only that, there is some skepticism. "When it comes to recovery drinks, the science doesn't always match the hype. Take those claims of precious electrolytes with a grain of salt. It's drilled into us by sports drinks that they're these magic bullets, but electrolytes are simply salt."

In the memoir I made the point that if you identify a new dimension, as Victoria's Secret did when it defined "everyday" luxury, you have to deliver. And it did—technically, functionally and emotionally. We'll have to see which of these new healthy beers really is healthy. That means a lot of sustained taste testing coming up. Someone's gotta do it.

15

WHAT IS THE
MOST POWERFUL
DIMENSION?

I **CAN'T LEAVE YOU** with a "how-to" guide for becoming a new-age marketer. Some sure way to twist a market-space into a new product or service that will change the world. There are no formulas. Only inspiration and courage. But there is one guiding thought I want to offer. It is about time.

Time present and time past
Are both perhaps present in time future,
And time future contained in time past.
If all time is eternally present
All time is unredeemable.
  T. S. Eliot, Four Quartets, Burnt Norton

Maybe the ultimate challenge for the modern marketer is to make time redeemable. Maybe that's how she or he saves the world.

Is time the ultimate dimension of our market-spaces? A powerful force that gets people to change their minds about what is valuable to them and what isn't?

Of course it is. What dominates our lives more than time? What drives us to use it, to save it, to savor it? When we are born we are given only so much of it. We can make more money but we can't make more time. I remember as a boy walking to church one morning thinking to myself I am going to close my eyes and wake up old. We all fear time and the death it ultimately brings. At our backs always is "time's winged chariot hurrying near."

I don't mean to be morose. And this is not high-minded theory. If you are a CEO or a market manager or strategist and you don't see the word "time" in the plan or proposal, throw it out. The big picture will be missing. And you need the big picture. When my McKinsey partner, Kenichi Ohmae, told me years ago that "convenience" would become a powerful dimension in the consumer space, he was really talking about time. Because convenience saves time. But the time dimension of a product or service can be much more subtle and complex. Obviously the value of a drug that lengthens your life or improves it is rooted in time. But there are many more products and services where time can become the dominant and winning dimension. I don't care if the product is a coffee cup—start asking questions about time. Should you shorten, or lengthen, the time it takes to use the product or experience? How can you explode the minutes, dissect the seconds?

Take a look at the website, slow-watches.com. A Swiss company now makes a watch with 24 hours on its face and only one hand. It urges potential buyers to "be slow." "We created a watch that allows you to experience time in an entirely different way." The company admits that it is a little harder at first to tell time accurately. But it is worth it, they say. Who cares about a couple of minutes? The new design prevents you from "getting stressed out by time." The watches are attractive. I might buy one. As they say, "Let's make time to bring back slow into our lives. Be slow."

I am not urging you to focus new product development on our ever larger market of aging people with lots of money. MIT's AgeLab has shown that doing so is a sure way to go out of business. Old people, it turns out, don't like to buy things that remind them they are old. They would rather suffer. (*Can We Live Longer But Stay Younger?*, The New Yorker, Adam Gopnik, May 13, 2019.) The challenge is time, not age.

When Netflix told its content providers to break the constraint of 30-minute television shows, it was asking them to rebundle time and the entertainment it provides. When it started to release a "season's" worth of content, it was making its products timeless and giving its customers a new freedom. When Patek Philippe tells potential customers to buy its expensive watches so they can pass them along to their children, it is using time and generations to redefine and increase their value. It's all about time.

A theme of this memoir has been that marketing can change how consumers measure value. For example, in the program we mounted to get people to control their blood pressure, we changed people's perception of the value of compliance. Instead of being about prevention, compliance became about love and taking care of your family. At McKinsey we changed our client's metric of value from insight to leadership. Yes, problem solving remained important, but more important, we said consulting helps you lead, not just analyze. Multi-stakeholder challenges such as drug development and public infrastructure will require new superordinate goals that redefine progress and value. Someday soon, I hope, we will redefine the value of infrastructure so people value it not in terms of pavement and public transportation but in terms of access. Why not get "there" in an instant? In all these examples, time is a major factor and different aspects of time can be used to redefine value.

There are things that come with time—reflection, love, dignity and courage. How can we make them come sooner, or more surely? How can we give people the courage to change? Because the other side of time is change. Recall Luc du Brabandere's admonition that we must change things twice, reality and perception. How do we do that? We can probably use AI to shorten feedback loops or accelerate learning, but how do you give customers confidence and willingness?

Time is a robust dimension. It has two ends and lots of spots along it where real value can be created, captured or shared. We all remember

Polaroid for bringing speed to the photography market. It may be that our new-age marketer should be looking for ways to slow things down rather than speed them up. To make them or their experience longer rather than shorter. At 73, I am interested in that idea. Maybe I should ask the publishers of this book to release it slowly, a chapter a week. Like a Dickens novel. But you can't make things too slow. If Keats' lovers on that Grecian urn never kiss, what does it matter?

Too many of us in marketing, talented and successful people, think time is an unforgiving and immalleable dimension. When it's gone it's gone. Maybe not. In a sense we get it back in dreams. How else? Don't be content with some skin cream idea that hides the scars of time. Strategists beware. You will need to use both your heart and head simultaneously. Edwin Land knew all about the technologies Polaroid owned, but more important, he listened to his daughter when she asked why she could not have a photo within seconds of taking it. Start with an astonishing premise. You may have read a short story by F. Scott Fitzgerald entitled "The Curious Case of Benjamin Button." In it, time is turned on its head. Benjamin is born an old little man in his 80s and then he begins to grow young. His experiences and relationships are entirely different from normal humans. What he values and loves. Invent a narrative about time that's as crazy as that. Then you might have something. Then you may be able to make men and women, young and old, true time travelers.

Play offense with time. Be aggressive in your thinking. Recall Herrick, "though we cannot make our sun stand still, yet we can make him run." Or be Freddie Mercury and Queen. When they tell you a song can be only three minutes long, make it six, and produce "Bohemian Rhapsody."

Let's, as modern marketers, help people redeem time. Make it more valuable. Learn from it. Enjoy it. Contemplate. See new things and new chances to make life better, every moment.

You will need inspiration as well as analysis. If you don't have a daughter or son to ask you fundamental questions, then maybe turn to literature.

Or music. Find that old record collection and pull out some favorites. I might grab Fleetwood Mac and listen to Stevie Nicks sing "Landslide."

I took my love and I took it down
I climbed a mountain and I turned around
And I saw my reflection in the snow covered hills
'Till the landslide brought me down

Oh, mirror in the sky, what is love
Can the child within my heart rise above
Can I sail through the changin' ocean tides
Can I handle the seasons of my life
I don't know

Well, I've been afraid of changin'
'Cause I built my life around you
But time makes you bolder
Children get older
I'm getting older, too

....

So, take this love, take it down
Oh, if you climb a mountain and you turn around
If you see my reflection in the snow-covered hills
Well, the landslide will bring it down, down
And if you see my reflection in the snow-covered hills
Well, maybe the landslide will bring it down
Well, well, the landslide will bring it down.

TRAVELOGUE

ANAGEMENT CONSULTING usually means lots of travel and I certainly did my share. It can be onerous, or it can be glamorous and fun. I must have stayed at the Four Seasons Boston over 300 times in my five years at BCG. The staff was incredibly good and I always got upgraded to suites. I probably stayed 200 nights at the Mayfair in London over the years. It was just around the corner from McKinsey's office and you could get there easily by subway from Heathrow. It wasn't the Dorchester or the Connaught, but it was comfortable and felt like home. I often fell asleep in the dining room, jet lagged, over a bottle of Chablis with Dover Sole. Then there were those little boutiques, like the Hotel Bel-Air in Los Angeles. Who stayed downtown back then? Or an incredibly chic place called L'hotel on the left bank. When it wasn't available (it once was an ice house and was very small), there was the Lancaster, just off the Champs-Elysees. The Okura in Tokyo was another of my favorites. They always greeted me by name even when my visits were infrequent. The tempura bar downstairs was the best. Its lobby was very much in the mid-century modern style. Just the opposite was the Dolder Grand in Zürich. Formal, almost severe, but impeccable. The dining room looked out on Lake Zürich. The most exotic meals I ever had were at a small ryokan in Kyoto. They lasted for hours. You sat on Tatami mats in robes while pretty Japanese ladies brought course after course to your room. Large gold carp swam in ponds outside the shoji screens. Sometimes you had no idea of what you were eating, but it was an adventure. My friend Ohmae arranged for me to take Pamela there once. Very unusual in the '80s. On that night, the pièce de résistance was a bowl of live baby squid. The trick was to wash them down quickly with saki. On one of my first visits to Hong Kong, I stayed at the Peninsula. They sent a Rolls Royce to pick you up at the airport. Think hot afternoons, cold sweaty drinks in that legendary lobby and James Bond. Thirty years of all that. Now we have three homes—in Connecticut, Long Island and West Palm—and we travel as little as possible to anyplace else.

Vladimir: Shall We Go?

Estragon: Yes, Let's Go.

They do not move.

(Beckett, Samuel, Act 2, Waiting for Godot.)

I'm not sure which of Marvin's birthdays we were celebrating in this picture. I'm pretty sure it was at La Cote Basque in New York. Marvin wasn't much for big parties, but he liked small gatherings like this. I'm the young guy on the left.

BILL'S
RECOMMENDATIONS

BOOKS

For Some, The Dream Came True, The Best From 50 Years of Fortune Magazine, selected and edited by Duncan Norton-Taylor (Astounding collection of articles from the '30s through the '70s by writers including Archibald MacLeish, James Agee, William Whyte and Daniel Bell.)

The Street Where I Live, by Alan Jay Lerner. If you want to understand creative collaboration (Lerner and Loewe), read this wonderful story of Broadway and musical theater.

Capitalism and Freedom, by Milton Friedman. This is the only book on economics you need to read. Yes, I'm biased.

Excellence, Can We Be Equal and Excellent Too?, by John W. Gardner. This book raised America's standards. Mine too.

Thinking in Systems, A Primer, by Donella H. Meadows.

Beautiful Women Ugly Scenes, by CDB Bryan. I read this on Cape Cod one summer a long time ago and it had an enormous effect on me.

Solving Tough Problems, An Open Way of Talking, Listening, and Creating New Realities, by Adam Kahane. Read this after you read Meadows.

The Opposable Mind, Winning Through Integrative Thinking, by Roger Martin. After Kahane.

Sound and Sense, An Introduction to Poetry, by Laurence Perrine. All of us need to read and feel poetry and the magic of language.

Elements of Style, by Strunk and White. Because so many people don't know basic grammar and can't write a strong, crisp sentence.

Adventures in the Screen Trade, A Personal View of Hollywood and Screenwriting, by William Goldman. Don't read this to understand Hollywood but to gain an appreciation for what "narrative" means and how to use scenes to make your writing more convincing.

Here is New York, by E.B. Whyte. The writing is extraordinary as is the portrait of New York in the late '40s.

The Life of Samuel Johnson, by James Boswell. Samuel Beckett kept this book, and only this book, on his desk.

The Reflective Practitioner, by Donald Schon. This was a giant book for me as I sought to understand how the best professionals think and act.

The Innovator's Dilemma, When New Technologies Cause Great Firms to Fail, by Clayton M. Christensen. By the '90s, most books on management were just rhetoric, but this book is the real deal. A well-researched classic.

The Herring Gull's World, A Study of the Social Behavior of Birds, by Niko Tinbergen. Because all business men and women should read at least one good book on sociology.

Animal Farm, by George Orwell. Just remember, "All animals are equal, but some animals are more equal than others."

Capitalism at Risk, Rethinking the Role of Business, by Bower, Leonard and Paine. There has been a lot of lousy thinking about this topic, but this book is well worth reading.

The Great Gatsby, by F. Scott Fitzgerald. My favorite novel. "Her voice is filled with money."

Great Expectations, by Charles Dickens. One of the greatest early novels. A poor country boy gets a mysterious gift and goes to London to learn about money and love.

PLAYS

Pack of Lies, by Hugh Whitemore. When does a lie become justified? This is the most compelling drama I have ever experienced. It's about a middle-aged London couple who find out that their neighbors are Soviet spies. Then they are convinced by British intelligence to counterspy on them. I saw it on the West End when it opened with Judi Dench in the lead role.

Waiting for Godot, by Samuel Beckett. There is no better play in which nothing happens. Don't read it; see it. It is actually hilarious as well as being very troubling.

MOVIES

Un homme et une femme – A Man and a Woman. Written and directed by Claude Lelouche, starring Anouk Aimée and Jean-Louis Trintignant. Unforgettable musical score by Francis Lai. I've seen it 20 times. A widow and widower meet, fall in love, but... Best ever love story on film.

Young Frankenstein, directed by Mel Brooks with an incredible cast that includes Gene Wilder, Peter Boyle, Marty Feldman, Teri Garr and Madeline Kahn. Side-splittingly funny.

Birdcage. Robin Williams at his best. Based on La Cage Aux Folles. Directed by Mike Nichols and written by Elaine May–the best comedy team ever.

Shakespeare in Love. Stoppard at his best. Won seven Academy awards including best screenplay.

Groundhog Day is a truly provocative comedy directed by Harold Ramis and starring Bill Murray, who finds himself caught in a time loop in a small town in western Pennsylvania.

Vertigo. Many think this is Hitchcock's best. Starring Jimmy Stewart and the incredibly beautiful Kim Novak. The shots of San Francisco are worth the price of the ticket. To say nothing of that Mark IX Jaguar sedan.

The English Patient. Nine Academy awards. Incredible acting by every member of the cast. Mesmerizing.

Roman Holiday. Because at least one movie with Audrey Hepburn has to be on the list. Gregory Peck isn't bad in it either. Filmed on location in Rome.

Guess Who's Coming to Dinner. Because of its time and storyline. And because at least one movie with Katharine Hepburn and Spencer Tracy has to be on this list. Along with that newcomer, Sidney Poitier.

Casablanca. Of course, because at least one movie with Bogart has to be on this list.

Lawrence of Arabia. Peter O'Toole is magnificent. I saw this movie when I was a student at Andover and hardly understood it.

Cabaret. Can there be a better musical? Liza Minelli and Joel Grey.

The Graduate was another masterpiece directed by Mike Nichols. It came out the year before I graduated from Harvard. Like Benjamin (Dustin Hoffman), I had no idea what I wanted to do. But no Mrs. Robinson, the incredibly seductive Anne Bancroft, showed up to help me see the future.

Good Morning Vietnam, released in the mid-'80s, is a black comedy about a disc jockey stationed in Vietnam. Robin Williams plays the disc jockey and most of his scenes are improvisations. Funny and not so funny if you were about to graduate from college and faced the draft. Best line: "It's hard to find a Vietnamese guy named Charlie." Buy the soundtrack. It has some great rock and roll.

Five Easy Pieces starred Jack Nicholson. It was a classic movie of rebellion in the early '70s. If you saw it, you remember the scene in the diner. "You want me to hold the chicken?" "I want you to hold it between your knees."

Coming Home. Both Jane Fonda and Jon Voight won best acting awards for their performances. It was an affecting movie about Vietnam and our obligation to serve our country. Voight played a paralyzed veteran. I got a high draft number and was never drafted. I still feel guilty. That's Pittsburgh for you.

The Godfather. Of course, epic and Italian.

Saturday Night Fever. Doo-wop becomes disco, but it's my childhood. The soundtrack is forever.

Being There. Peter Sellers and Shirley MacLaine. The film can be described as a dark comedy. It was based on a much darker novel written by Jerzy Kosiński. It recounts how a gardener becomes a nominee for President of the United States. "I like to watch."

An American in Paris. What a movie. What dancing. What dancing by Gene Kelly. I wanted to be an astronaut when I was young. Then I wanted to be a dancer like Kelly. And get girls like Leslie Caron.

Her. A man, Joaquin Phoenix, falls in love with a software program with a sexy voice.

A Beautiful Mind. A movie about the mathematician John Nash, his mental illnesses, and him winning the Nobel prize.

If I look at the whole list, I realize that I like movies, but really love screenplays with intriguing premises.

MUSIC

I have always loved listening to music, of all kinds. We can divide music into several categories and they reflect my background and experiences.

Doo-wop. Growing up in the '50s and '60s in western Pennsylvania means one thing: rock and roll. I was nuts about it; it was made for dancing. The Moonglows, The Flamingos, Chuck Berry, Frankie Lymon and the Teenagers, Little Anthony and the Imperials, The Skyliners,

The Coasters and The Five Satins. The list could go on forever and would certainly include Elvis even though he wasn't really doo-wop.

In Pittsburgh, you got exposed to the **big bands** and the **crooners**. On the radio, you heard Frank Sinatra, Dean Martin, Sammy Davis, Eydie Gorme, Nancy Wilson, Dinah Washington and Tony Bennett. I liked them all. They could sing and you could understand their words. In the early '80s, Tony Bennett came to Heinz Hall in Pittsburgh. I took my mother backstage to meet him. She was thrilled. Her picture with him held a special place in our home. Afterwards, he, I, Mario and Abby Mann (author of *Judgment at Nuremberg*) went to Tambellini's for dinner—the best Italian place in town.

I wasn't exposed to much **classical music** growing up. At Andover, I spent a few weekends with family friends and started to listen to their collection of LPs. I must have listened to Dmitri Shostakovich's 7th Symphony (Leningrad) 20 or 30 times. It told me a story about Russia and war. After that I gradually became familiar with the great violin concertos and American composers such as Aaron Copland, who painted pictures for me of the American landscape as did George and Ira Gershwin. In New York, I started to listen to opera. At first to Montserrat Caballé and then to the extraordinary voice of Maria Callas. Eventually and for several years, I took a very nicely located box at Carnegie Hall and entertained friends and clients there.

I did a little amateur theater at Harvard. Mostly minor roles in musicals, so Broadway lured me to its many stages when I joined McKinsey. I walked over there one night when I first settled in the city and bought a ticket from a scalper to see *A Chorus Line*. After that I was hooked. Pippin, Company, Chicago, lots of good stuff. I liked the old musicals more, particularly Lerner and Loewe (*My Fair Lady, Camelot, Gigi*). From there, it was an easy step to Cole Porter and Noël Coward. And, of course, there was the unique and wonderful *West Side Story*.

Then there is what could be called "**contemporary**" music. For me, that covered music from the mid-'60s to the present. The '60s in Cambridge were the start of folk music. Dylan, Baez, Joni Mitchell. But then, The Beatles were established. I walked into my room at Quincy House one morning after a class and my roommate, who played drums in a local band, was going crazy over a new guy named Jimi Hendrix. Soon I was too, as well as over a singer named Janis Joplin. One year after Harvard, there was a little event called Woodstock that brought us groups like Santana and Crosby Stills Nash and Young. There were so many good groups. Jefferson Airplane was one of my favorites. So were The Lovin' Spoonful, Cream, Talking Heads, The Fifth Dimension and (I'll admit it) The Bee Gees. Ray Charles, George Benson, Van Morrison. Noel Pointer, Donna Summer, Michael Jackson, Eric Clapton, David Bowie and Grace Jones, and at least 50 more were all my favorites and all quite different.

POETRY

To be honest, I haven't read a new poem in years. I takes time to understand a poem. And it takes life, with all its ups and downs, to embrace it into your heart and mind. But Kris, my talented publisher, tells me readers have indicated they would like to see a list of poems I would recommend. So here are some poems, or parts of them, I carry around in my head and recall from time to time to help me put things in perspective.

The first is quoted at the beginning of this memoir. Try to imagine yourself in the early part of the 17th century. Here is this young poet, John Keats, reading a new translation of Homer. He describes how he now sees, literally sees, seafaring adventures described by Homer two centuries earlier very differently. And he manages to do this within the constraints of a sonnet, a Petrarchan sonnet no less. I know the poem by heart. I recite it to myself often. I marvel at the power of its images. There's the explorer Cortez, for example, standing on a high ridge staring at an ocean he has just discovered with his men below him trying to figure out what he sees. It is the perfect poem to start a memoir on the visual aspect of marketing.

The second poem on my list is T. S. Eliot's "The Love Song of J. Alfred Prufrock."

> Let us go then you and I
> With the evening spread out against the sky
> Like a patient etherized upon a table.

Dudley Fitts read it to us in the basement of Bullfinch Hall my last year at Andover. He didn't try to teach it. He just wanted us to hear it, knowing that a decade or two later we would better understand the issues—love, sex, death—the protagonist was trying to grasp. "And the women come and go, talking of Michelangelo." A sophisticated, complicated, modulated and truly modern poem.

The third poem, "A Slumber Did My Spirit Seal," could not be more different than the first two. It demonstrates the power of one-syllable words and simple verse. A man loses his wife or lover. He never expects her to die, or to die first. When Pamela discovered last year she had breast cancer, guess what poem came into my head? Wordsworth, around 1700:

> A slumber did my spirit seal,
> I had no human fears,
> She seemed a thing that could not feel,
> The touch of earthly years.

> No motion has she now, no force.
> She neither hears nor sees,
> Rolled round in earth's diurnal course,
> With rocks and stones and trees.

Love and death have inspired a couple other poems on my list. First, a poem entitled Funeral Blues by Auden that is desperate and sad.

> Stop all the clocks, cut off the telephone,
> Prevent the dog from barking with a juicy bone,
> Silence the planes and with a muffled drum,
> Bring out the coffin, let the mourners come.....
>
> He was my North, my South, My East and West,
> My working week and my Sunday rest,
> My noon, my midnight, my talk, my song.
> I thought that love would last forever, I was wrong.

Love and death inspired the only poem by Shakespeare on my list, To Autumn. I like structure in poetry and this sonnet's structure and imagery are perfect, as is the last couplet:

> That time of year thou mayst in me perceive
> When yellow leaves or none or few do hang upon these boughs
> that shake against the cold,
> Bare ruined choirs where late the sweet birds sang....
>
> This thou perceivist which makes thy love more strong,
> To love that well which thou must leave ere long.

Not all the love poems on my list are sad. Robert Herricks's Upon Julia's Clothes is pure celebration of ladies and beauty by one of the original poet bad boys. And one word is a poem all by itself.

> Whenas in silks my Julia goes,
> Then then (methinks) how sweetly flows
> That liquefaction of her clothes.
>
> Next, when I cast mine eyes, and see
> That brave vibration each way free,
> O how that glittering taketh me!

There was a pop tune in the '40s or '50s I'm convinced was inspired by Herrick. "Standing on the corner watching all the girls go by."

One of my favorite poems is about seduction, failed seduction! John Donne's "The Flea" is a short poem in which a man tries to convince a woman to sleep with him because, he argues, both have been bitten by the same flea. "And in this flea," he says "our two bloods mingled be." Rather than say no, she squashes the flea and elicits one of the great lines of bathos in literature.

> Cruel and sudden hast thou since
> Purpled thy nail in blood of innocence?

Donne later in his life wrote several great metaphysical poems that were about God and religion (No man is an island, ask not for whom the bell tolls, etc.), but when he wrote "The Flea," he was quite a rogue and great reading for a young man at Harvard.

My taste in poetry is not sophisticated. I will even admit to reading Rod McKuen. And one of his poems from Stanyon Street makes my list. Here's the end of it.

You've filled completely
this first November day
with Sausalito and sign language
canoe and coffee
ice cream and your wide eyes,
And now unable to sleep
because the day is finally going home,
because your sleep has locked me out
I watch you and wonder at you.
I know your face by touch when its dark
I know the profile of your sleeping face
the sound of your sleeping.
Sometimes I think you were all sound
kicking free of covers
and adjusting shutters
moving about in the bathroom
taking twenty minutes of our precious time.
I know the hills
and gullys of your body.
The curves
the turns.

I have total recall of you
and Stanyon Street
because I know it will be important later.

It's quiet now.
Only the clock
moving toward rejection of tomorrow
breaks the stillness.

That's pretty bad, isn't it? But sometimes in the '60s it worked on a first date.

Poems are not just words. They are often about a place and time, and even a moment. The two that stand out for me are Emily Dickinson's "I Heard a Fly Buzz When I died":

> With Blue—uncertain—stumbling Buzz—
> Between the light—and me—
> And when the Windows failed—and then—
> I could not see to see.

And Robert Browning's "My Last Duchess." In this poem, the speaker, a duke, admits to murdering his wife. Ironically, he admits this to a man representing a woman who might be his new wife!

> That's my last duchess painted on the wall,
> Looking as if she were alive.

The Duke explains the jealousy that provoked his decision.

> Oh, sir, she smiled no doubt, whene'er I passed her,
> but who passed without
> Much the same smile? This grew. I gave commands ;
> Then all smiles stopped together.

Now we get to those big poems about the universe and the meaning of things. One is Blake's The Tiger.

Tiger tiger burning bright
In the forest of the night.
What immortal hand or eye
Could frame thy fearful symmetry?

I am convinced that the imperfect rhyme of eye and symmetry is deliberate. Nature is all the more powerful in its imperfection. "Did he," he asked, "who made the lamb make thee?"

Then there is William Butler Yeats' masterpiece, The Second Coming. It asks the basic question, is civilization heading toward heaven or hell.

Turning and turning in the widening gyre
The falcon cannot hear the falconer;....

somewhere in the sands of the desert
A shape with lion body and the head of a man,
A gaze blank and pitiless as the sun, Is moving its slow thighs,
while all about it
Reel shadows of the indignant desert birds.
The darkness drops again; but now I know
That twenty centuries of stony sleep
Were vexed to nightmare by a rocking cradle.
And what rough beast, its hour come round at last,
Slouches towards Bethlehem to be born?

For Yeats' question, I have no answer except to fall back on love and add to this list, Mathew Arnold's "Dover Beach."

Listen! You hear the grating roar
Of pebbles which the waves draw back, and fling,
At their return, up the high strand,
Begin, and cease, and then again begin,
With tremulous cadence slow, and bring
The eternal note of sadness in.

The Sea of Faith
Was once, too, at the full, and round earth's shore
Lay like the folds of a bright girdle furled.
But now I only hear
Its melancholy, long, withdrawing roar,
Retreating, to the breath
Of the night wind, down the vast edges drear
And naked shingles of the world.

Ah, love, let us be true
To one another! For the world, which seems
To lie before us like a land of dreams,
So various, so beautiful, so new,
Hath really neither joy, nor love, nor light,
Nor certitude, nor pease, nor heal; for pain;
And we are here as on a darkling plain
Swept with confused alarms of struggle and flight,
Where ignorant armies clash by night.

Or, if you want a shorter answer. Try that line from the band, Kansas,

All we are is dust in the wind.

Okay, there is one last poem I need to cite. "Slimbo the Big Foot Reindeer." I wrote it myself. Well, I adapted it from another song about a reindeer named Rudolf. You see Pamela has big feet–size nine at least. Somehow they fit with her long legs. At Christmas time we sing this song together. I am particularly proud of the last line.

Slimbo the big foot reindeer had a very shiny nose
And if you ever saw her You would say she had big toes.
All of the other reindeers used to laugh and call her names,
They wouldn't let poor Slimbo play in any reindeer games.

Then one slippery Christmas Eve, Santa came to say,
Slimbo with your magnopeds, Won't you pull my great big sled?
Now all the other reindeers laugh and shout it out with glee,
Slimbo the big foot reindeer you should have a pedigree!

I missed my calling.

WINES

There are too many to list. Pamela and I really enjoy Italian reds, particularly Barolos and Brunellos. But a big Cabernet from California is always good with a steak or a hamburger. There are lots of great Bordeauxs, of course, but our favorites tend to be Pomerols. Our favorite whites come from Alsace. Pinot gris. For breakfast for almost a decade, Pamela and I drank nothing but Elephant beer, a Danish brew made by Carlsberg. But in the last few years, we have become big fans of India Pale Ales. Not the citrus-flavored ones. Rather the high-alcohol, hoppy ones. Our favorites are made by Sixpoint Brewery in Brooklyn. Try the Bengali and Resin.

RECIPES

Iceberg Wedges with Blue Cheese Dressing

TOTAL: 20 MIN

6 SERVINGS

1 cup crumbled Roquefort cheese	1/2 teaspoon finely grated lemon zest
2/3 cup sour cream	1 tablespoon plus 2 teaspoons chopped flat-leaf parsley
2/3 cup mayonnaise	
1/4 cup fresh lemon juice	Salt and freshly ground pepper
2 scallions, minced	6 large wedges of iceberg lettuce (1 1/2 heads)
1/2 teaspoon chopped thyme	
	6 radishes, very thinly sliced

1. In a bowl, using the back of a fork, lightly mash the Roquefort with the sour cream and mayonnaise. Stir in the lemon juice, scallions, thyme, lemon zest and 2 teaspoons of the chopped parsley. Season the blue-cheese dressing with salt and pepper.

2. Set the lettuce wedges on a platter. Spoon a generous amount of the blue-cheese dressing over each lettuce wedge. Top with the sliced radishes and the remaining 1 tablespoon of chopped parsley. Serve.

FOOD & WINE, March 2004 issue

LAMB and WHITE BEAN CHILI   NYTimes
                                    Wed. Feb. 15, 2012

2 T. olive oil
1 lb. ground lamb   Plain yogurt (pref. by sheeps milk)
Kosher salt + black pepper   or sour cream, for serving
1 onion finely chopped   Lime wedges (or sliced scallions)
2 poblano peppers, seeded + diced (or 2 sm. green peppers)   for serving
1 sm. bunch cilantro, cleaned
4 garlic cloves, finely chopped
2 sm. jalapeños, seeded, if desired, and finely chopped
2 T. chile powder, plus more to taste
1 t. gr. coriander
1 t. gr. cumin
1½ T. tomato paste   Serves 4-6
3½ c. cooked white beans (homemade or canned)

Heat oil in a soup pot over med.-hi heat.
Add lamb + cook, breaking up w/ a fork, until
well browned, ≈ 5 min. Season w/ ½ t.
each of salt + pepper. Transfer meat to a
paper-towel-lined plate.
    Add onion + poblano peppers to pot. Cook
until vegetables are softened, 5-7 min.
Finely chop 2 T. of cilantro stems + add to
pot. Stir in the garlic + jalapeño and cook
2 min. Add chile powder, coriander + cumin
+ cook 1 min. Stir in tomato paste + cook until
it begins to brown.
    Return lamb to the pot. Stir in 4 c. water,
beans and ¼ t. salt. Simmer over med-lo
heat for 45 min. Add more water if chile
becomes too thick. Taste and adjust
seasonings if necessary. Ladle into bowls
+ top w/ dollop of yogurt + squeeze of lime.
Garnish w/ chopped cilantro leaves.

Mashed Potatoes and Leeks with Thyme

3	pounds russet (baking) potatoes (about 6)	3/4	stick (6 tablespoons) unsalted butter
6	leeks (white and pale green parts only), chopped, washed well, and drained	1	tablespoon fresh thyme leaves, minced
		1	cup milk
		1/2	cup heavy cream

In an 8-quart kettle combine potatoes with cold water to cover by 2 inches. Bring water to a boil and simmer potatoes until tender, 35 to 45 minutes.

While potatoes are cooking, in a heavy skillet cook leeks in 4 tablespoons butter over moderately low heat, stirring occasionally, until softened. Stir in thyme and salt and pepper to taste.

Drain potatoes in a colander and return to kettle. Dry potatoes over low heat, shaking kettle, 1 minute. Cool potatoes just until they can be handled and peel. While potatoes are still warm, force through a ricer into a large bowl. In a small saucepan heat milk and cream until mixture just comes to a boil. Stir leeks and milk mixture into potatoes and season with salt and pepper. Spread potato mixture in a buttered 4-quart shallow baking dish. Chill potato mixture, covered, 1 day.

Preheat oven to 350° F.

Dot potato mixture with remaining 2 tablespoons butter and bake, covered with foil, in middle of oven until heated through and butter is melted, about 15 minutes. Serves 8.

GOURMET, November 1996 issue

a memoir

Curried Lamb Potpie

ACTIVE: 1 HR, TOTAL: 3 HR 15 MIN

6 SERVINGS

Accarrino's unconventional potpie is filled with coconut-spiked curried lamb. "The flavors remind me of dishes I've had in Sicily, so I'd pour a juicy Sicilian Nero d'Avola," says Lindgren. Look for the 2006 Gulfi Nerobaronj, her pick, or the 2010 Tenuta Rapitalà.

PASTRY

1 1/2 cups all-purpose flour

1/2 teaspoon salt

1 stick cold unsalted butter, diced

1/4 cup ice water

CURRY

3 tablespoons extra-virgin olive oil

2 pounds trimmed boneless lamb shoulder, cut into 3/4- inch cubes

Salt and freshly ground pepper

1 medium onion, chopped

2 teaspoons curry powder

2 1/2 tablespoons all-purpose flour

1/3 cup dry white wine

2 cups chicken stock

2 cups peeled butternut squash, cut into 1-inch dice (10 ounces)

2 cups chopped Tuscan kale

1 medium carrot, chopped

1 cup unsweetened coconut milk

2 tablespoons chopped parsley

1 large egg lightly beaten with 1 teaspoon of water

1. MAKE THE PASTRY. In a food processor, pulse the flour and salt. Add the butter; pulse to the size of peas. Sprinkle the ice water over and pulse until the pastry starts to come together. On a work surface, gently knead the pastry a few times. Shape into a disk, wrap in plastic and refrigerate until firm, 1 1/2 hours.

2. MAKE THE CURRY. In a Dutch oven, heat 1 tablespoon of the oil. Season the lamb with salt and pepper and add half to the casserole. Cook over high heat until browned on 2 sides, about 3 minutes. Using a slotted spoon, transfer the lamb to a bowl; repeat with 1 more tablespoon of oil and the remaining lamb. Pour off the oil in the casserole.

3. Add the remaining 1 tablespoon of oil and the lamb to the casserole. Add the onion and cook over moderate heat, stirring, until softened. Add the curry powder and cook, stirring, for 1 minute. Stir in the flour, then slowly stir in the wine until smooth. Add the stock and bring to a boil, stirring, until thickened, 1 minute. Cover and simmer over low heat until the lamb is very tender, 1 hour.

4. Add the squash, kale, carrot and coconut milk to the casserole and simmer over moderately low heat until the vegetables are tender, 10 minutes. Season with salt and pepper. Stir in the parsley and let cool.

5. Preheat the oven to 375°. Spoon the curry into a buttered 8-by-11-inch baking dish. Brush the dish rim with beaten egg. On a lightly floured surface, roll out the pastry to a 14-by-12-inch rectangle. Fold the pastry in half, unfold it over the curry, and gently press onto the edge of the dish. Brush with beaten egg; cut 4 small steam vents in the top.

6. Bake the potpie for 40 minutes. Raise the heat to 450°; bake for 20 minutes longer, until the pastry is browned and cooked through. Let rest for 20 minutes, then serve.

Accarrino and Lindgren's new book is SPQR: Modern Italian Food and Wine.

FOOD & WINE, October 2012 issue

MUSHROOM, PORK AND VEAL LOAF W/Thyme.   J+W.
Febr. '89
1½ c. chicken stock or canned broth   p. 132-3
1 oz. (≈ 1c.) dried wild mushrooms, such as porcini or shitake, rinsed
¼ c. long-grain white rice   1 t. fr. gr. pepper
~~½ lb. fr. mushrooms~~   1½ lbs. ground veal
~~6 T. butter~~   1 lb. ground pork (≈ 20% fat)
~~1 med. onion, chopped~~   2 eggs, beaten
½ lb. fr. mushrooms
6 T. butter
1 med. onion, chopped
½ c. heavy cream
3 T. minced fr. thyme or 2 t. dried
2 garlic cloves, minced
2 t. salt   6-8 servings

In a sm. saucepan bring the chicken stock to a boil. Put the dried mushrooms in a sm. heatproof bowl + pour on the stock. Let stand, covered, til softened, ≈ 30 min. In a sm. saucepan, bring 1½ c. water to a boil, add the rice, cover + cook over lo heat til softened, ≈ 12 min. Drain + set aside. Remove the soaked mushrooms, reserving the liquid. Strain the liquid thru a fine sieve or several layers of dampened cheesecloth. In a food processor, combine the soaked mushrooms + the fresh mushrooms; finely chop.
In a lge skillet, melt the butter over lo heat. Add the onion + chopped mushrooms + cook, stirring frequently, til lightly browned, ≈ 8 min. Stir in the reserved stock, the cream, cooked rice, thyme + garlic. Cook, stirring frequently, til mixture is reduced + very thick, ≈ 5 min. Remove fr. heat, stir in salt + pepper + let cool to rm. temp. Preheat oven to 350°. In a lge bowl, combine the veal, and pork. Add the mushroom mixture + the eggs + mix well. Transfer to a lge shallow baking dish + form into a flat loaf.
Bake the meat loaf til a thermometer inserted in the center registers 160°, ≈ 1 hr + 10 min. Let the loaf rest on a rack for ≈ 10 min. before slicing + serving.

Spicy Macaroni and Cheese

1 1/2	cups finely chopped onion		cayenne to taste if desired
2	large garlic cloves, minced	1	pound elbow macaroni
1 1/2	tablespoons minced pickled jalapeño chilies, or to taste	1 1/2	cups coarsely grated Monterey Jack (about 6 ounces)
1	teaspoon ground coriander		
1 1/2	teaspoons ground cumin	1 1/2	cups coarsely grated extra-sharp Cheddar (about 6 ounces)
1/2	stick (1/4 cup) unsalted butter		
1/4	cup all-purpose flour		
4	cups milk	1 1/2	cups fresh bread crumbs
	a 28-ounce can plum tomatoes, the juice discarded and the tomatoes chopped and drained well	1 1/3	cups freshly grated Parmesan (about 1/4 pound)

In a large heavy saucepan cook the onion, the garlic, then jalapeños, the coriander, and the cumin in the butter over moderately low heat, stirring, until the onion is softened, stir in the flour, and cook the mixture, stirring, for 3 minutes. Add the milk in a stream, whisking, bring the liquid to a boil, whisking, and whisk in the tomatoes. Simmer the mixture for 2 minutes and add the cayenne and salt and pepper to taste.

In a kettle of boiling salted water cook the macaroni for 6 to 7 minutes, or until it is barely al dente, drain it well, and in a large bowl combine it with the tomato mixture. Stir in the Monterey Jack and the Cheddar and transfer the mixture to a buttered 13- to-14- by 9-inch shallow baking dish or 3-quart gratin dish. In a bowl stir together the bread crumbs and the Parmesan, sprinkle the mixture evenly over the macaroni mixture, and bake the macaroni and cheese in the middle of a preheated 375°F. oven for 20 to 25 minutes, or until it is golden and bubbling. Serves 6 to 8.

GOURMET, September 1991 issue

BAGNA CAUDA   Gourmet
                                                October '91
5 garlic cloves, mashed to a paste   p. 198
7 garlic cloves, sliced thin
1⅓ c. olive oil
6 oz. flat anchovy fillets, drained + chopped
½ stick (¼ c.) butter

Accompaniments:
   Red bell peppers, sliced
   celery, cut into sticks
   fennel bulbs, sliced
   boiled potatoes, quartered

                        Makes ≈ 1¾ c.

BAGNA CAUDA   Cuisine
   (Garlic-butter-olive oil-anchovy dip for crudités)   May 1982

3/4 c. olive oil
½ c. butter
12 cloves garlic, finely chopped
1 can (2 oz.) anchovy fillets, well drained, coarsely chopped

(Serve w/ 6 c. bite-cut assorted crudités)

                        Makes ≈ 1½ c. dip

VEAL MILANESE   8-22-01 NYTimes

3 eggs
2 T. finely grated Parmesan
1½ T. chopped parsley
1 c. flour
1-2 c. fine bread crumbs made w/stale (not toasted) crust on country bread
4 lrge handfuls arugula
2 sm. or 1 lrge, very ripe tomatoes, roughly chopped
½ sm. red onion, thinly sliced
extra virgin olive oil
juice of 1 lemon
4 veal chops, w/bones, pounded very thin (no thicker than pie crust)
Corn oil
1 lemon, cut into wedges (for serving)

1. In a small bowl, whisk together eggs, cheese and parsley. Season generously with salt and pepper. Pour into a large, shallow bowl or tray. Spread flour in a second shallow bowl and bread crumbs in a third. Set aside near stove.

2. In a large mixing bowl, combine arugula, tomatoes and onion. Sprinkle with olive oil and lemon juice.

Season with salt, and toss until leaves are coated. Dressing should be assertive and lemony. Set aside.

3. Working one at a time, press each veal chop into flour on each side, then pat it off so that there is just a fine dust on veal. Dip chop into egg, coating both sides, and letting as much drain off as possible. Lay chop in bread crumbs, tapping it gently to make sure it gets coated, but ever so thinly. Flip it over, and coat the other side. Layer chops between waxed paper or parchment as you go.

4. Heat oven to 175 degrees, and place a baking sheet on middle rack. Place a sauté pan large enough to fit 2 chops over medium-high heat. Pour in enough corn oil to generously cover base of pan. When oil shimmers (it should be very hot so the veal seizes immediately), add a chop and sauté until browned, 2 to 3 minutes. Turn and brown other side. Transfer to baking sheet, and keep warm in oven. Repeat with other chops.

5. To serve, place chops on each of four large plates. Place a large handful of salad on top of each, making sure each gets enough tomatoes and onion. Serve with a wedge of lemon, for squeezing over the meat.

Yield: 4 servings.

NEW YORK TIMES, 8-22-2001

Pumpkin Pie

Otto Seelbach, a member of the Louisville Seelbach Hotel family, who knew good food, told me years ago that a pumpkin pie should "cry"-that is, small teardrops of moisture should rise to the top after the pie rests for a while. In other words, a delicious pumpkin pie must be moist and luscious. This is the pumpkin pie that cries.

Makes One 9-Inch Pie

Old-Fashioned Pie Crust, unbaked (recipe follows)

1	cup canned pumpkin	1/2	teaspoon ground ginger
1	cup heavy cream or evaporated milk	1/4	teaspoon freshly grated nutmeg
3	eggs	1/4	cup brandy
1	cup (packed) light brown sugar		Chilled Bourbon Custard (p. 175)
1	teaspoon ground cinnamon		or whipped cream, as accompaniment

1. Preheat the oven to 400°. Cover pie crust with aluminum foil and weigh down with dried beans. Place the pie pan on the bottom rack of the oven and bake for 15 minutes, or until the crust is almost dry and lightly colored. Remove the beans and the foil and set the partially baked crust aside to cool for a few minutes.

2. Meanwhile, measure the pumpkin into a large bowl. Gradually whisk in the cream. Add the eggs one by one, whipping until well blended.

3. Combine the sugar with the spice and beat them into the pumpkin mixture. Add the brandy and mix well. Spoon the filling into the partially baked crust.

4. Place the pie on the lowest shelf of the oven and bake for 8 minutes. Reduce the oven temperature to 350° and continue to bake until a knife inserted in the middle comes out clean, 40 to 45 minutes longer. Serve warm or cold, with chilled Bourbon Custard and whipped cream.

FOOD & WINE

FUDGY BROWNIES

Z+W
Mar. '90
p. 62 (pic. p. 60)

2 sticks (8 oz.) butter
4 oz. unsweetened chocolate, coarsely chopped
2 c. sugar
4 eggs
1 t. vanilla extract
1 c. flour
½ t. salt
1 generous c. coarsely chopped walnuts or pecans (≈ 3 oz.)

Makes 35 brownies

Preheat oven to 350°. Lightly grease a 13 x 9 x 2" metal or ceramic baking pan.
In a lge saucepan heat the butter over mod-lo heat til half melted. Add the chocolate + stir til butter + chocolate are completely melted + combined. Remove fr. heat and stir in the sugar w/a wooden spoon til incorporated.
Using the wooden spoon, beat in the eggs, 1 at a time, stirring after ea. addition til eggs are fully incorp'd and the chocolate mixture is shiny. Stir in the vanilla. Add the flour + salt all at once + mix til blended. Stir in the chopped nuts.
Scrape batter into the prepared pan. Bake for 30 min., or til brownies are slightly firm to the touch + a cake tester inserted in center indicates brownies are moist. Let cool completely in pan. Cut into 35 bars.

Sometimes clouds make beautiful sunsets. We'll see. Not long after I finished this memoir, Pamela and I learned she had breast cancer. It was in an early stage and her surgery went well. Her latest check-up made us feel very fortunate. There is that saying that wise people "treat each day like a precious gift." We have tried to do that. We will do so more gratefully going forward.

Working with Bill and Pamela has been one of the highlights of my career. They are the truly rare people who are sincere, grateful for what they have, who mean well, love each other and have both the ability and inclination to change the world for the better.

If you enjoyed *Marketing Saves the World*, would you mind taking a minute to write a review on Amazon? Even a short review helps, and it'd mean a lot to me.

If someone you know would benefit from reading about architecture, market-spaces (not places!) and dimensions, social marketing, multi-stakeholder solutions, marketing and strategy, please tell them about this book. I think the more people who read this book, the bigger positive impact this book will make in the world.

Universities, organizations, bloggers, influencers and others looking to make the memoir and documentary available to their audiences are welcome to contact me at **kris@firmsconsulting.com**.

Finally, if you would like to receive bonus updates on related content and receive a complimentary episode from the accompanying documentary series, *The Bill Matassoni Show*, go to **www.marketingsavestheworld.com**.

The world awaits. Go make change happen!

Kris Safarova
CEO, Firmsconsulting

ABOUT THE AUTHOR

BILL MATASSONI

After graduating from Harvard Business School, Bill joined Porter Novelli, a small consulting firm that was pioneering the concept of social marketing. His first client was the National High Blood Pressure Education Program. "Instead of selling soap I learned how to sell and keep selling people the benefits of compliance. Not easy. You can't scare them forever. We needed to convince them that treating their blood pressure was an act of love," says Bill. His next client was United Way of America, where he soon became VP of Marketing. He produced and wrote a nationally televised advertising campaign that featured every NFL team. "Two years out of HBS and I'm writing football spots. But the players did a great job and the ads ran for years."

Then, to his surprise, Bill got a call from McKinsey. The recruiter asked him if he was interested in creating a marketing program for the "preeminent" consulting firm. He said no. They called back a few months later. This time he said yes. It was time, Bill thought, to re-enter the private sector. And to broaden his experience selling ephemeral things. "There was no job description. I decided not to try to impose some sort of marketing strategy worldwide. Instead I found 20 partners in different countries who were ready to make things happen and had something to say." Two years after joining McKinsey, Bill was elected a partner. For almost two decades, he was responsible for advancing McKinsey's reputation and protecting its brand. In doing so, he worked closely with many of his colleagues worldwide. He was also responsible for McKinsey's internal communications. This included the creation of McKinsey's systems to manage and disseminate its practice knowledge.

In 1999, Bill left McKinsey to join Mitchell Madison Group, a strategy consulting firm. He helped to take the firm public through its sale to USWeb/CKS. He then joined The Boston Consulting Group, where he headed for over five years a group responsible for integrating innovation, marketing and communications. Bill worked closely with several of BCG's thought leaders to develop their ideas and turn them into consulting assignments. After retiring from BCG he founded The Glass House Group, a consulting firm that helps professional services firms on branding and marketing issues.

Bill is a graduate of Phillips Andover (1964), Harvard College (B.A. Literature, 1968) and Harvard Business School (M.B.A., 1975). He and his wife, Pamela, live in New Canaan, Connecticut in a glass house designed by Philip Johnson (the Boissonnas house). The house and their renovation of it have been featured in several magazines and newspapers including Town and Country, Metropolitan Home, and The New York Times. Their current interests include contemporary Chinese painting (black ink on paper) and "as much good wine as their budget and health can tolerate."

For many years, Bill was on the board of trustees of United Way of America and United Way International. He is now on the board of trustees of First Book and a senior advisor to Ashoka, an organization that invests in social entrepreneurs. He remains interested in the management and marketing of professional services firms and social marketing. "Marketing," he says, "can help us make real progress against complex, multi-stakeholder challenges. Don't become a finance guy. You can have much more impact and fun as a marketer."

ABOUT THE PUBLISHER

THE STRATEGY MEDIA GROUP

At the Strategy Media Group, we believe in the power of critical thinking, creativity, and storytelling to teach our clients to solve mankind's toughest problems. Our mission is producing original long-form content to empower a loyal, hardworking, inspiring, well-meaning and ambitious worldwide audience to solve the most important problems and, as a result, make a positive and meaningful impact on the world.

Our clients make a difference because they aspire for more than that which society had intended for them. They do not confuse aspiration for ambition. They choose the latter. They act.

We provide a full range of content development, financing, marketing and distribution services for wholly owned educational programs, documentaries, feature films, and podcasts teaching business strategy, problem-solving, critical thinking, communication, leadership and entrepreneurship streamed in >150 countries 24/7 through feature-rich Apps and websites.

At any given time >1,000 unpublished episodes are in post-production. Our digital properties include **StrategyTraining.com**, **StrategyTV.com** and **FirmsConsulting.com**. Our apps include Strategy Training, Strategy TV, Strategy Skills and Bill Matassoni A Memoir.

In addition, we own some of the world's most popular business strategy and case interview podcast channels with >3.5 million downloads and counting, and the world's largest business strategy OTT platforms with >5,000 episodes of original programming distributed on iOS, Android, Roku and Apple TV.

We have financed, packaged or distributed more than 45 premium programs through our wholly owned OTT platforms, including "The Electric Car Start-Up," "The Digital Luxury Atelier," "The Gold Miner," "Competitive Strategy with Kevin P. Coyne," "The Bill Matassoni Show," and we try to focus on social causes like championing the rights of disenfranchised workers.

We take an equity ownership positions in businesses we are documenting to produce programming for our platforms. Such as a gold miner, electric car start-up, luxury brands start-up, and new age cosmetics start-up.

Our programming is analytically and conceptually deep, in that we dig into the numbers and details to help you understand the economics at work, and help you replicate our thinking. "The US Marketing Entry Study" and "The Corporate Strategy & Transformation Study," with >270 videos each, are programs used worldwide to understand the nuances of restructuring a retail bank and turning around a troubled power utility.

In the scripted space, we create original content combining education with entertainment to deliver business teachings.

Our publishing arm releases original books on strategy, business and critical thinking, such as "Marketing Saves the World" by Bill Matassoni, McKinsey's former senior partner and world-wide head of marketing and "Succeeding as a Management Consultant."

We teach business and critical thinking skills to children and young adults, with original and entertaining novels and programming merging entertainment and business training. We believe children and young adults will have a formidable advantage in life if they start learning to think like a strategy partner early in life. STEM skills should be complemented with critical reasoning skills. It should be strategy, science, technology, engineering and mathematics.

We invest in and have exposure to the world's fastest growing market segments and market geographies, including the BRICS. Our subscribers include senior government officials, and leaders of industry and consulting firms, all the way to the executive committee members of the world's leading consulting firms.

We work with eminent leaders such as ex-McKinsey, BCG, et al. partners who plan, produce and/or host all our programming. The type of content we produce does not exist anywhere else in the world and is hosted exclusively on our platforms.

Kris Safarova is the Presiding Partner of Firmsconsulting.com, the world's largest strategy streaming OTT channel. She was born in Samara City, the Russian Federation. She received a Dipl. in Music with a concentration in Classical Piano from DG Shatalov Music College, a B.Comm from UNISA, cum laude with highest distinction and an MBA from Ivey Business School, University of Western Ontario, on the deans list with highest distinction, where she was President of the Public Sector Club and Editor of the Public Sector Journal. Prior to obtaining her business degrees, she worked in management consulting and post-MBA she was a banker and consulting engagement manager in Toronto. Prior to consulting Kris was a master classical concert pianist and official representative of the Russian Federation who toured Europe. She joined Firmsconsulting.com as a Partner, Corporate Finance in 2015 and was appointed Presiding Partner in 2016.

RECEIVE ACCESS TO AN EPISODE
FROM THE BILL MATASSONI SHOW:

www.MarketingSavesTheWorld.com

RECEIVE ACCESS TO EPISODES FROM
OUR VARIOUS TRAINING PROGRAMS:

www.FIRMSconsulting.com

GENERAL INQUIRIES:

support@firmsconsulting.com

COLLABORATION/PARTNERSHIP
INQUIRIES:

kris@firmsconsulting.com

BULK ORDER REQUESTS /
GROUP MEMBERSHIPS:

support@firmsconsulting.com

SUGGEST A GUEST FOR OUR
PODCAST CHANNELS:

support@firmsconsulting.com